Series / Number 07-025

MAGNITUDE SCALING
Quantitative Measurement of Opinions

MILTON LODGE

State University of New York at Stony Brook

SAGE PUBLICATIONS   Beverly Hills   London

For information address:

SAGE Publications, Inc. 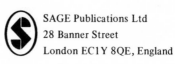 SAGE Publications Ltd
275 South Beverly Drive 28 Banner Street
Beverly Hills, California 90212 London EC1Y 8QE, England

International Standard Book Number 0-8039-1747-3

Library of Congress Catalog Card No. L.C. 81-52923

FIRST PRINTING

When citing a professional paper, please use the proper form. Remember to cite the
correct Sage University Paper series title and include the paper number. One of the
following formats can be adapted (depending on the style manual used):

(1) IVERSEN, GUDMUND R. and NORPOTH HELMUT (1976) "Analysis of Variance." Sage University Paper series on Quantitative Application in the Social Sciences,
07-001. Beverly Hills and London: Sage Pubns.

OR

(2) Iversen, Gudmund R. and Norpoth. Helmut. 1976. *Analysis of Variance*. Sage
University Paper series on Quantitative Applications in the Social Sciences, series no.
07-001. Beverly Hills and London: Sage Pubns.

CONTENTS

MAGNITUDE SCALING
Quantitative Measurement Of Opinions

MILTON LODGE
*State University of New York
at Stony Brook*

1. INTRODUCTION TO THE MAGNITUDE SCALING OF SOCIAL JUDGMENTS

The measurement technique most commonly used by social and behavioral scientists to determine the direction and strength of people's beliefs and preferences is one or another form of category scaling in which a respondent rates an item or expresses a judgment by selecting one of a fixed number of options. As a procedure for scaling impressions, category scaling dates back to at least 150 B.C. when Hipparchus used a six-point scale to judge the brightness of stars. A variety of 2-, 3-, 5-, 7-, and 9-point category scales are widely used in the social sciences today to measure almost every conceivable social-psychological impression. However, despite its long history and widespread contemporary use for measuring strength of opinion, category scaling has a number of serious weaknesses.

First of all, information is lost because of the limited resolution of the categories. Even when respondents can clearly distinguish between two objects, category scaling forces them to make similarity-difference judgments and place items judged to be "more or less" alike into the same category. The greater the discrepancy between the true range of the stimuli and the fixed range of the category scale, the poorer the resolution of the categories. For this reason categorical judgments may be thought of as qualitative rather than quantitative.

A second, related problem is that category scales represent only an ordinal level of measurement, thereby denying researchers legitimate access to many of the powerful statistical methods based on interval assumptions which are available today for the description, prediction, and modeling of relationships. Many researchers, not content with ordinal data, assign integers to the categories, treat them in interval fashion, and use more powerful statistical techniques than are warranted.

And finally, by offering a fixed number of categories, however few or numerous, the researcher is inadvertently affecting the response. Whereas the true change of social stimuli varies over time from domain to domain and individual to individual, the range of categorical options remains set, sometimes artifactually constraining judgments, at other times providing a too expansive range, and only on occasion, fortuitously, matching fixed to true range.

Queries about the character of the intensity measures developed by category scaling procedures are hardly trivial, as experience with decades of attitude research consistently reveals that the degree of correspondence between measures of attitude and behavior is typically low to moderate. While crude measurement is certainly not the sole explanation for the disappointing degree of correspondence between social attitudes and behavior, what makes the measurement problem so important is that as a consequence of poor measurement, we cannot know whether our failure to find a closer correspondence between attitude and behavior results from weaknesses in our theoretical formulations or deficiencies in our measurements.

Recent advances in the theory and practice of psychophysics now provide a viable alternative to category scaling and promise a dramatic improvement in the measurement of social opinion. Paralleling explicitly the methodology developed over the past 20 years for the ratio scaling of such sensations as the loudness of sound, brightness of light, sweet and sour tastes, heaviness of lifted weight, pleasant and foul odors—virtually all aspects of the five senses—it now appears possible and feasible to apply this methodology originally developed for the magnitude scaling and validation of physical stimuli on sensory continua to the ratio scaling and validation of social stimuli on social-psychological dimensions.

The aim of this volume is to describe the magnitude scaling approach in sufficient detail to provide students of the social and behavioral sciences with the conceptual wherewithal to appraise the relative costs and benefits of this approach and to spell out step-by-step procedures for the scaling and validation of magnitude scales of social opinion in experimental and survey research.

One final word before we begin. This volume is presented as a practical guide to the magnitude scaling of social judgments. The measures and methods are simple and straightforward, so disarmingly simple and direct, in fact, that many of us who worked hard learning how to tease a pattern out of statistically noisy data initially find it hard to accept that any social-scaling method can produce such lawful relations as are commonly obtained from magnitude scaling. What is central, then, are the whys and wherefores—the logic of magnitude scaling and the interpretation of results. To provide the conceptual underpinnings we will move back and forth between sensory and social psychophysical scaling, for the parallelism between the two is not merely a heuristic or analogy, but, rather, the basis for the criterion tests used to validate social scales: Social scales should behave as lawfully as do scales of physical sensations.

2. OVERVIEW OF PSYCHOPHYSICS

To set this magnitude scaling methodology in perspective, let us first outline the paradigm for sensory psychophysical scaling, for the logic, measures, and procedures developed for quantifying physical stimuli on a sensory continuum are virtually identical to the methods, tests, and analyses employed in the magnitude scaling and validation of social-psychological judgments.

Numeric estimation—matching numbers to one's strength of impression—is the simplest, most direct, and most widely used method for constructing ratio scales of sensation. In the classic psychophysical experiment, subjects are presented with a series of sensory stimuli (say, varying light intensities) one at a time in random order across a wide range of stimulation and are instructed to give numbers to the perceived brightness of each stimulus relative to the first (light intensity), called a reference.

Prototypical instructions read:

You will be presented with a series of (light) stimuli in irregular order. Your task is to tell how intense they seem by assigning numbers to them. Let the first (light) stimulus be your reference. Give it any number that seems appropriate to you, keeping in mind that some of the stimuli will be (brighter) than the reference and others will be (dimmer) than the reference. Assign a number to each of the stimuli such that it reflects how much weaker or stronger it is compared to the first stimulus: The brighter it is compared to the reference, the bigger your number response; the (dimmer) it is compared to the reference, the smaller your number response. There is no limit to the range of numbers you may use. Try to make each number match the intensity (of light) as you see it [adapted from Stevens, 1975: p. 30].

So, if a given light seemed 2 times brighter than the reference light, the subject would give a number twice as large as that assigned the reference light; if another light was judged 10 times brighter than the reference, one would give it a number 10 times larger; if one-third as bright, a number one-third as large, and so on for a range of light intensities. What is characteristic of the magnitude estimation procedure is that all judgments are made explicitly relative to a reference, typically, to a low-intensity or middle-level stimulus. What is critical is that the individual be free to match the continuous response measure under his or her control to the perceived intensity of the stimuli.

Although the number system is relatively well-learned, the explicit act of matching numbers to the perceived strength of stimuli is unfamiliar, so many magnitude scaling studies begin with a simple training exercise, such as judging the apparent length of lines. The reader is urged to try this task himself, for it represents the basic psychophysical approach and plays an important role subsequently in the magnitude scaling of social impressions. The exercises will provide step-by-step instructions for magnitude scaling, practice in graphing and analyzing relationships, and equally important, establish the critical analogy between the scaling of judgments of physical stimuli on a sensory continuum and the scaling of judgments of social (nonmetric) stimuli on social-psychological dimensions.

Exercise A: Numeric Estimation of Metric Stimuli

Preparation of a Work Sheet. In these exercises you will need a pencil, sheet of lined paper, and hand calculator with a Common Log (base 10) and Exponential (10^X) function.

Divide a piece of lined paper lengthwise into five columns. Label the first column "Line Length Stimuli" and write the letters A through L down the column, one letter per line. Label the second column "Numeric Estimates," the third column "Logs of Numeric Estimates," the fourth column "Arithmetic Mean of the Logs," and the fifth column "Geometric Mean."

Magnitude Scaling Instructions. Here are a set of line lengths, labelled A to L.

Note that some of the lines are longer than the first line, A, and some are shorter. The first line is your reference. Let us give it the number 50. Your task is to say how much longer or shorter the lines are compared to the first line by giving each line a number compared to 50. The longer a line appears to be compared to the reference line, the bigger the number you will give it compared to 50. The shorter a line compared to the first line, the smaller the number you should give it compared to 50.

No rulers, please. Just give each line a number that seems appropriate: If a line seems to be about twice as long as line A, give it a number about two times bigger than 50, that is, about 100. If a line appears about one-fourth as long as your reference line, give it a number about one-quarter of 50, or about 12.

Preparation of Response Data. Write your numeric estimate for each line length in the second column of the work sheet. Line A = 50. If at all possible, have 5 to 10 people carry out this scaling exercise: Enter their numeric estimates also in column 2. Averaging over a number of people will smooth the curve and provide a much firmer basis for assessing results. (Ideally, of course, each stimulus would be presented several times to increase reliability and in different orders to eliminate order effects.)

If, as hoped, you were able to collect numeric estimates from a group of people, hereafter called subjects, three steps on a hand calculator will compute an average of the magnitude responses to each stimulus:

(1) Take the common log (base 10) of each subject's numeric response to each line length stimulus and enter the log values in column 3. (Logarithms to base 10 are most appropriate to psychophysical data and this log function is built into hand calculators with scientific notation.)
(2) Calculate the arithmetic mean of the logs for each stimulus. Enter this value in column 4.
(3) Exponentiate (raise to the power of 10) the means of the logs (10^X on your hand calculator) to obtain the geometric mean. The geometric mean (the antilog of the mean of the logs) is the appropriate measure of central tendency with magnitude data. Enter the geometric mean for each stimulus in column 5.

If you were not able to obtain numeric estimates from a group of subjects, simply place your single numeric estimate of each line length stimulus in column 5 of the work sheet.

Plotting Psychophysical Relationships. A simple, quick, and informative way to determine whether the magnitude of people's judgments is proportional to the magnitude of the stimuli is to plot the relationship on a logarithmically ruled graph. Here the geometric means (or your numeric responses) should be plotted on the *log* Y axis against the actual millimeters of line length on the *log* X axis.

A blank sheet of logarithmic graph paper (called a log-log or ratio-ruled graph) is reproduced in Figure 1 for you to plot this relationship.[1] Mark the actual value of each line length stimulus on the log-ruled horizontal axis: A = 50 mm, B = 26 mm, C = 74 mm, D = 4 mm, E = 98 mm, F = 38 mm, G = 2 mm, H = 14 mm, I = 18 mm, J = 64 mm, K = 8 mm, and L = 86 mm. Place the geometric mean (or your numeric estimate) for each stimulus on the log-ruled vertical axis and pencil in the data points on Figure 1.

Because equal distances on a logarithmic scale mark off equal ratios, a straight line on ratio-ruled coordinates represents a power function: Subjective magnitude (of apparent length) grows proportionately with proportional increases in stimulus magnitude (of actual length). The predicted exponent for numeric estimates of metric stimuli on a quantitative continuum such as line length is unity—a function of 1.0, $Y = X^{1.0}$—which is drawn as a 45° line on Figure 1. Actually, there will certainly be some statistical variability ("noise") in these data, but the points should still fall close to the 45° line, even for a single respondent. Draw a best-

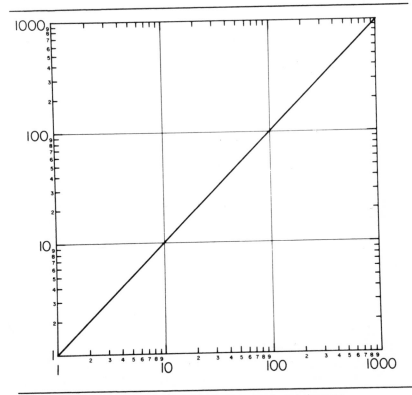

Figure 1: Logarithmically ruled graph for plotting magnitude judgments.

fitting line through the points you obtained. If, as expected, your plot is reasonably described by a straight line, the numeric estimates represent ratio judgments and the obtained scale would be described as a ratio (or power) scale. Compare your results to the plot in Figure 2.

Figure 2 displays the results of a similar training exercise in magnitude scaling obtained from a sample of 375 respondents interviewed in 1974 by the University of Michigan's Survey Research Center for the Tanenhaus and Murphy survey of support for the U.S. Supreme Court. The geometric means of the numeric estimates are plotted as a function of nine line length stimuli in ratio-ruled coordinates. The solid line represents the theoretically expected exponent of 1.0. The empirically obtained regression exponent is .988 ($Y = X^{.99}$).

This close, linear match of numeric estimates to actual line length confirms that the respondents are using this magnitude response measure to make ratio judgments. When, as here, the function is linear on log-log coordinates, the numeric response estimates represent ratio-level judg-

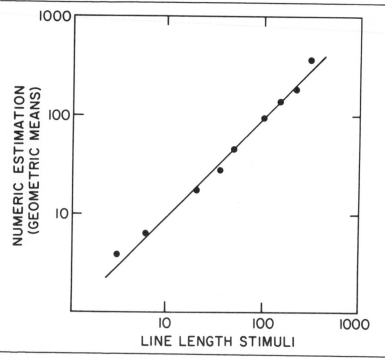

Figure 2: Numeric estimates plotted as a function of line-length stimuli on log-log coordinates. Each point represents the geometric mean averaged over 375 respondents of the Murphy-Tanenhaus national survey. The solid line drawn through the plot represents the theoretical exponent of 1.0. (From Lodge et al., 1975; reprinted by permission.)

ments and the researcher can—after carrying out a set of criterion tests described later—treat the numeric estimates as psychophysically valid ratio estimates and then get on with the critical job of testing functional hypotheses of the type: Y is a function of X^b.

The Power Law

The results of hundreds of such numeric estimation experiments establish that human observers are capable of using numbers to make proportional judgments of stimulation levels for virtually all aspects of the five senses. When these numeric estimates of the perceived strength of sensory stimuli are logged, averaged, and plotted directly against the objectively measured stimulus values on log-log coordinates, the points typically fall on a straight line. The principle underlying this linear relationship in ratio-ruled coordinates is simple and lawful—*equal stimulus ratios pro-*

duce equal subjective ratios. This is the essence of the psychophysical power law governing human impressions of most physical sensations (Stevens, 1957) and is probably the most strongly supported law of human judgments in psychology today (Cliff, 1973). The power law may be represented as

$$Y = kX^b,$$

or, for our purposes,

$$\psi = R = kS^b,$$

where ψ is subjective magnitude, one's impression of stimulus magnitude, R is the magnitude of response, S is the magnitude of the stimulus, b is the exponent which characterizes the relationship, and k is a constant of proportionality. When the power law is transformed into logarithms, the equation becomes linear:

$$\log R = b \log S + \log k,$$

since,

$$\begin{aligned} \log Y &= \log kS^b \\ &= \log k + \log S^b \\ &= \log k + b \log S. \end{aligned}$$

In its logarithmic form the function is similar to the linear relationship of an interval scale, and the derived scale may be most accurately described as a proportionality scale.[2]

Exercise B: The Category Scaling of Metric Stimuli

To show the close similarity but dramatic differences between category and magnitude estimation procedures for measuring the strength of one's judgments, it would prove helpful if the reader were now to scale the line length stimuli using a standard category scale. The act of *categorizing* metric stimuli (here lines) is an odd thing to do—given thousands of years of effort in developing precise measures of length—but a worthwhile exercise nonetheless, as it will illustrate basic relationships between different scaling procedures and provide experience in graphing relationships between types of scales. Also, keep in mind that we are interested in developing a scaling method for measuring people's *judgments* of stimuli, not the stimuli themselves. The advantage here of using metric stimuli is that they can be measured accurately, and different types of scaling procedures can be compared directly to *known* parameters.

The conversion from magnitude to category scaling is straightforward, requiring only that subjects now be told to restrict their responses to a set of arbitrarily fixed numbers, rather than be told to freely match numbers directly to the strength of their impressions. The line length stimuli above may be scaled on this conventional variant of a 7-point category rating scale:

(1)	(2)	(3)	(4)	(5)	(6)	(7)
Short			Medium			Long

On the reverse side of your work sheet, write the letters A through L down the left side and label this column "Category Scale Ratings." Now categorize each line length by assigning it the most appropriate number between 1 and 7. If you are able to collect responses from a number of people, enter the arithmetic mean of their categorical responses to each stimulus in a second column labelled "Mean Category Rating."

It is no easy task forcing a 49:1 range into a restricted set of categories. Not as simple, perhaps, as the numeric estimation procedure or, as we shall see, as informative. For the moment, make note of the fact that you were forced to place stimuli which were discernibly different into the same category. Unable to record relative magnitudes, the subject is forced to make qualitative (ordinal) judgments—the 2 mm and 4 mm lines, for example, may have been categorized as "short," the 86 mm and 98 mm lines as "long"—whereas in the numeric estimation task you could discriminate between them by giving each stimulus a relatively smaller or bigger number response.

At this juncture it would prove helpful if you were to plot the line length stimuli, measured in millimeters, against the categorical judgments on ordinary, linear-linear graph paper. A blank linear-linear graph is reproduced in Figure 3. Assuming, as is the custom, that the categories represent equal intervals, 7 equally spaced intervals have been marked off on the Y axis. Place the arithmetic mean of the categorical responses on the axis. On X, place the actual values of line length stimuli: 50, 26, 74, 4, 98, 38, 2, 14, 18, 64, 8, and 86. Now plot the relationship.

Many such plots appear in the psychophysical literature (Stevens and Galanter, 1957). The characteristic function for categorical responses of a quantitative continuum is curvilinear. We have not drawn an expected curve on this linear-linear graph because the degree of curvature is dependent in unpredictable ways on the order and spacing of stimuli, the

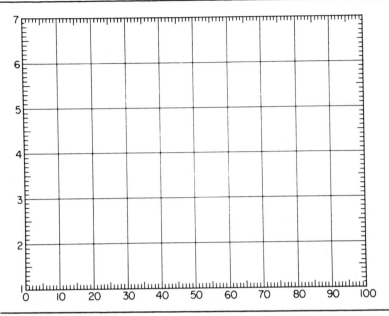

Figure 3: Linearly ruled graph for plotting categorical responses.

number of categories, and the true range of the stimuli. For this moderate 49:1 stimulus range, the best guess-estimated function is a gentle, negatively accelerated slope.

The nonlinear relationship between category scales and quantitative variables in linear-linear coordinates has serious methodological and substantive consequences for the social and behavioral sciences which we will explore in detail in later sections of this volume. But first, to illustrate some basic problems with category scaling, let us take a closer look at your categorical judgments. Some of the line length stimuli approximate a linear progression: The 2, 14, 26, 38, 50, (64), 74, 86, and 98 mm lines are incremented by 12 mm each. How well do your categorical judgments reflect these intervals? Probably not too well, for the characteristic curve relating category scales to intervally spaced physical stimuli means that increments added to low stimulus values have a greater impact on categorical judgments than do the same increments when added to high stimulus values—hence the initially steep acceleration of the curve and its tailing off at the high end of the scale. The general finding from numerous comparisons of category scales to intervally spaced metric stimuli reveals that categorical judgments do not routinely reflect intervals (Shinn, 1974). On the other hand, the numeric estimation method typically does represent the interval spacing of stimuli (as shown in Figure 2).

Another comparison: The 2, 4, 8, 16, (38), and 64 mm lines approximate a geometric progression. How well do your categorical judgments track this doubling of stimuli? In all likelihood not too well, for category scales have rarely been shown to reflect either the relative or absolute magnitude of stimuli. How well do your numeric estimates represent this geometric sequence? Your numeric estimate of the 4 mm line ought to be twice that of the 2 mm line and double again for the 4:8, 8:16, 16:38, and 38:64 pairs of stimuli.

The use here of metric stimuli highlights some of the basic problems inherent in all forms of category scaling, regardless of the type of stimulus, whatever the format of the category scale, whether the investigator imposes 3, 5, 7, 9, 11, 22, 100, or 1000 points, whether the continuum is represented by a broken or continuous line, designated by numbers, symbols, or adjectives. Category scaling costs information: Although one may perceive differences in stimulus intensity, category scaling makes it impossible to express their relative or absolute value.

Exercise C: Comparison of Magnitude to Category Scales

One final comparison before turning to the scaling of social judgments, this between your numeric and categorical judgments. When magnitude scales are compared to category scales in direct matches against metric stimuli on a quantitative continuum, the relationship between types of scales is almost invariably curvilinear. This finding deserves emphasis for it represents something of a law of human judgments. This effect can be demonstrated graphically, and readers are urged to plot the relationship between their numeric and categorical responses.

A semilog graph is reproduced in Figure 4. The X axis is linear, the Y axis logarithmically ruled. Mark your categorical response to each line length stimulus (or the arithmetic mean if you have group data) on X. Now place the geometric mean of each numeric response (or your numeric estimate) on the logarithmically ruled Y axis and pencil in the points. Predictably, the relationship will be markedly curvilinear.

When, as here, magnitude scales are compared to category scales in direct matches against a known metric, the relationship between scale types is characteristically curvilinear, typically concave downward—magnitude scales are almost invariably found to be superior in providing quantitative information about the intensity of people's judgments.[3] Numerous such scale confrontation studies demonstrate that category scaling results in: (1) the loss of significant portions of information, (2) ordinal level response data, (3) the misclassification of stimuli and respondents, and (4) because the number of categories and the assignment of numbers to categories are arbitrary, indeterminate regression co-

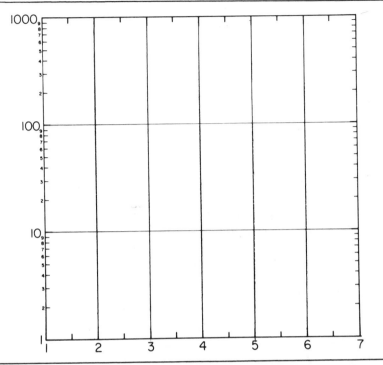

Figure 4: Semilog graph for plotting magnitude judgments against categorical judgments.

efficients. A rule of thumb: *The greater the disparity between the subjective range of the stimuli and the arbitrary range of the category scale, the greater the deviation from interval assumptions, the greater the loss of information, and the greater the distortion of response.* The long and the short of it is weak measurement and weak hypothesis and theory testing.

Numeric estimation, on the other hand, offers distinct advantages:

(1) Given the simple instruction to match numbers (or as we shall see, any of 30 continuous response measures) to the strength of one's impressions, the average person can make proportional judgments about the intensity of most sensory continua.

(2) Because magnitude scaling places no investigator-imposed restraints upon the response measures, respondents are able to express and investigators record judgments as precise as possible: If an individual is capable of judging a stimulus as two, three, four, or more times stronger than another, that ratio information can be conveyed through magnitude scaling.

(3) These magnitude scaling procedures produce proportional, ratio-preserving measures of opinion strength, thereby providing re-

searchers with legitimate access to powerful statistical tools such as regression analysis for testing quantitative hypotheses.

Before turning to the validity of these claims, let us first illustrate the applications of the numeric estimation procedure to the magnitude scaling of social judgments. The logic and methods for the magnitude scaling of social stimuli on a social-psychological dimension are the same as those outlined earlier for the magnitude scaling of one's impressions of physical stimuli on a sensory continuum. Typically, words and phrases describing social objects or events are substituted for the physical stimuli.

One of the earliest and most influential attempts to apply sensory psychophysical methods to the scaling of social judgments was carried out by Sellin and Wolfgang (1964) in their study *The Measurement of Delinquency*. Juvenile Court judges, parole officers, and college students (the archetypical representative of Everyman) were instructed to assign numbers to various phrases describing criminal offenses such that their numeric estimate matched their judgment of the seriousness of such crimes as "trespassing," "stealing and abandoning a vehicle," the "theft" of various sums of money, "arson," "rape," and "murder," each stimulus presented under a variety of circumstances from verbal threats to gunpoint with different degrees of injury to the victim. Sellin and Wolfgang uncovered a remarkable degree of consensus among experts in the criminal justice system and students as to the perceived severity of crimes.

This study has been replicated many times over in the United States, Canada, and England on judges, police officers, prison inmates, prosecuting attorneys, and of course students (Figlio, 1976), and most recently by Figlio (1978) for the U.S. Bureau of the Census as part of the 1977 Crime Victimization Survey which had a national sample of 54,000 people make numeric estimates of more than 200 descriptions of criminal offenses. Rather than simply describe the methodology and review the findings, readers are again urged to participate in a modified version of this study.

Exercise D: Numeric Estimation of Social Stimuli

Prepare a work sheet with five columns, just as you did for the scaling of line lengths, the first column headed "Criminal Offenses" with the letters A to 0 down the page, the other columns labelled "Numeric Estimates," "Logs of the Numeric Estimates," "Arithmetic Mean of the Logs," and "Geometric Mean." Once again you are encouraged to collect responses from a group of subjects, ideally the same ones who made numeric estimates of the line length stimuli. Although impressions of social stimuli are noisier than are impressions of sensory stimuli, 10 subjects should suffice to produce an interpretable curve.

Scaling Instructions. The instructions for this social scaling task could simply substitute "statements describing crimes" for "line lengths" in the earlier set of instructions, "more serious" and "less serious" crimes for "longer" and "shorter" lines. Procedurally, verbal descriptions of criminal offenses are treated *as if* they were line lengths, noises, light intensities, or any other physical attribute of a sensory continuum. The bureau's instructions read:

> I would like to ask your opinion about how serious YOU think certain crimes are.
>
> The first situation is, "A person steals a bicycle parked on the street." This has been given a score of 10 to show its seriousness. Use this first situation to judge all others. For example, if you think a situation is 20 TIMES MORE serious than the bicycle theft, the number you tell me should be around 200, or if you think it is HALF AS SERIOUS, the number you tell me should be around 5, and so on. There is no upper limit; use ANY number so long as it shows how serious YOU think the situation is. If YOU think something is not a crime, give it a zero.

Three practice items were presented, and then a subset of 25 items of the total number of 204 were presented in different versions. Here is a set of items which you are encouraged to scale. Write your numeric estimate for each item in column 2 of your work sheet:

COMPARED TO THE BICYCLE THEFT
SCORED AT 10, HOW SERIOUS IS:

A. A person using force, robs a victim of $10. The victim struggles and is shot to death.

B. A person disturbs the neighborhood with loud, noisy behavior.

C. A person steals property worth $1000 from outside a building.

D. A parent beats his young child with his fists. The child requires hospitalization.

E. A man forcibly rapes a woman. Her physical injuries require hospitalization.

F. A person steals property worth $10 from outside a building.

G. A person, using force, robs a victim of $10. No physical harm occurs.

H. A person plants a bomb in a public building. The bomb explodes and 20 people are killed.

I. A person steals property worth $10,000 from outside a building.

J. A person smuggles heroin into the country.

K. A person steals property worth $50 from outside a building.

L. A factory knowingly gets rid of its wastes in a way that pollutes the water supply of a city. As a result 20 people become ill but none requires medical treatment.

M. A person steals an unlocked car and later abandons it.

N. A person steals property worth $100 from outside a building.

O. A person, using force, robs a victim of $10. The victim is hurt and requires hospitalization.

Analysis of Numeric Estimates. Follow exactly the methods described earlier for analyzing your numeric matches to line length stimuli. If you collected responses from a number of subjects: First, take the log of each subject's numeric estimate of each stimulus and enter this log value in column 3. Second, calculate the arithmetic mean of the logs for each stimulus and enter the mean in column 4. Then, exponentiate the mean of the logs to obtain the geometric mean. Now compare your estimates to the magnitude scale values obtained from the bureau's sample of 54,000: Item A = 964, B = 25, C = 150, D = 501, E = 657, F = 38, G = 163, H = 1578, I = 240, J = 427, K = 63, L = 431, M = 97, N = 78, 0 = 319.

This simple procedural shift from physical to social stimuli highlights two basic problems endemic to all social scaling *regardless of method*, whether a researcher is asking subjects to make ordinal, interval, or ratio judgments: one, the ambiguity of the social stimuli and the scalar dimensions, a problem we take up in ensuing sections, the other, of immediate concern, *the lack of known metric properties for social stimuli*. Whereas estimates of line lengths can be plotted directly against actual millimeters of length, or estimates of loudness regressed against objectively measured decibels of sound pressure to determine the psychophysical relationship between the magnitude of sensation and the magnitude of stimulation, the estimates of the social stimuli cannot be plotted against the actual value of the social stimuli, because the true value of social stimuli is unknown. Their scalar properties—whether nonsense, nominal, ordinal, interval, or ratio—are generally the object of inquiry. The problem can be phrased in very practical terms: Lacking an objective measure of stimulus values, where are we to place the social stimuli on the X axis?

Unable to compare social judgments directly against a known, objectively measured metric, social scientists are typically forced to rely on one form or another of "face" or "construct" validity. For example, returning to the crime stimuli, one could have subjects also category scale the items and then plot their numeric estimates as a function of categorical ratings on a semilog graph, as done in Figure 4 for the line length stimuli. You may test this for yourself by categorizing the items on a 7-point scale and plotting the categorical means against the geometric means of your numeric estimates on Figure 4. The expected result would be markedly nonlinear, simply indicating that the magnitude and category scales are curvilinearly related, but not telling you which scaling method better represents the perceived severity of crimes.

A second, indirect validity test would be to compare the estimates of groups whose judgments are expected—on the basis of some prior knowledge or theory—to differ or covary in predictable ways. Sellin and Wolfgang took this approach in a series of analyses comparing the magnitude judgments of juvenile court judges to parole officers and students. When the numeric estimates of one group were plotted on log-log coordinates against the estimates of the other, they uncovered a remarkable degree of consensus between groups—that is, a straight line on ratio-ruled coordinates and strong product-moment correlations—thereby bolstering the construct validity of the scale. You may plot your numeric estimates against the geometric means obtained by the Bureau of the Census on the log-log coordinates of Figure 1 to determine how well your judgments match those of the national sample.

A third approach—this too carried out by Sellin and Wolfgang—better approximates the direct comparisons found in the classical psychophysical experiment.[4] Note that five of the criminal offenses (Items F, K, N, C, I) involve the theft of $10, $50, $100, $1000 and $10,000 under the same non-violent condition. By plotting the numeric estimates of the seriousness of each theft on the Y axis against the actual dollar figures on the X axis, we would expect a linear function on log-log coordinates *if* the perceived seriousness of thefts is a power function of dollar amounts stolen.

Figure 5 displays the relationship uncovered between adjudged seriousness and the theft of money from two studies—Sellin and Wolfgang's (1964) study (squares) and Figlio's (1977) study for the Bureau of the Census (circles). In both instances the relationship is well-described by a straight line on ratio-ruled coordinates: Numeric estimates of the seriousness of theft grow as a power function of the dollar amount stolen. Before discussing this relationship, you are encouraged to plot onto Figure 5 your numeric estimates of Items F, K, N, C, and I on log Y against the respective $10, $50, $100, $1000, and $10,000 values on log X.

The points on the Sellin and Wolfgang plot are the pooled estimates (geometric means) of 150 college students, while those from the bureau's study are averaged over several thousand "real world" adults, so your plot will not as likely be as smooth. Nonetheless, given the consensus found in numerous studies for judgments of the severity of crimes, a best-fitting line drawn through your points should be linear. What is more, the slope of your regression line will predictably fall close to the two reported in Figure 5.

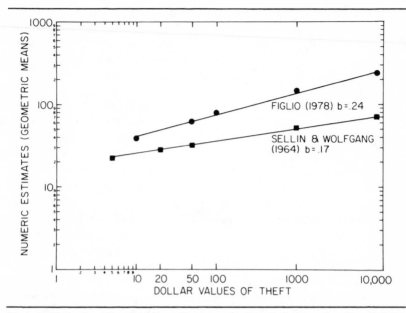

Figure 5: Numeric estimates of the seriousness of crime plotted as a function of dollar values of theft on logarithmic coordinates for two studies. Each point on the plot represents the geometric mean averaged over 150 students for the Sellin and Wolfgang study (squares) and averaged over several thousand people in Figlio's 1977 Bureau of the Census study (circles).

One of the most interesting aspects of this plot and the primary rationale for magnitude scaling is the slope of the lines. The regression coefficient (obtained by ordinary least squares) using the logs of the stimulus and response variables from the bureau's study is .27, and that recovered by Sellin and Wolfgang is .17. Numerous replications report slopes within this range, most hovering around .25. On log-log coordinates the regression coefficient can be interpreted as a direct expression of the relationship between variables. Thus, the slope of .27 uncovered for the national sample means that for one theft to be considered twice as serious as another, the dollar amount stolen must be about 13 times larger ($13^{.27} = 2$).

These and other relationships analyzed by Sellin and Wolfgang provide a convincing demonstration of the construct validity of their scale and by implication of the magnitude scaling method itself. Although all "face" and "construct" validity tests are more or less equivocal, the fit of data to expectations obtained in this study was strong enough to spark interest in the application of magnitude scaling to social attitudes.

Stevens (1966a, 1972) ably reviews the early effort in social psychophysical scaling. A partial list of social opinion scales derived from numeric estimation include: *the prestige of occupations* (Kuennapas and Wikstroem, 1963, with Swedish subjects; Dawson and Brinker, 1971, with Americans), *social status* as a function of income, years of formal education, and occupation (Hamblin, 1971, 1974; Shinn, 1969, 1974; Coleman and Rainwater, 1978); *strength of religious attitudes* (Finnie and Luce, 1960); *moral judgments* (Ekman, 1962); susceptibility to illness as a function of *life stress* (Holmes and Rahe, 1967); the *importance of political offices* (Ekman and Kuennapas, 1963, for Swedish subjects; Shinn, 1969, and Lodge et al., 1974, with Americans); *liberalism-conservatism* (Kuennapas and Sellin, 1964); *political dissatisfaction* (Welch, 1972); *national power* (Shinn, 1969); *national conflict and cooperation* (Corson, 1970); as well as numerous scales measuring the strength of likes and dislikes for food, drink, and the like (Stevens, 1972). These magnitude scaling studies demonstrate that the average experimental subject can, given proper instruction in the use of numeric estimation, make proportional judgments about the perceived intensity of many social stimuli on various social psychological dimensions.

What is particularly noteworthy about these studies is the type of stimuli and breadth of social-psychological dimensions successfully scaled to date: Ranging from such metric stimuli as dollars of income and years of formal education in scales of social status, to such simple titles as "carpenter" and "college professor" in scales of occupational prestige, to their combination in multivariate descriptions of the sort "Mr. _____ is an electrician who earns $10,500 a year and has an eighth grade education."

At this point you, the skeptical reader, may well be as ready as were early critics of psychophysics (Luce, 1959) to challenge the claim that the numeric estimation procedure produces ratio scales. It is, you might argue, one thing to match numeric estimates against metric stimuli to obtain a function which, if linear on log-log coordinates, confirms that people are making ratio judgments, but something else again, something qualitatively different, to lay claim to a ratio scale when the stimuli are nonmetric. Unlike such stimuli as dollars of theft or dollars of income or years of education, all of which come with numbers attached, most social stimuli, like the rape, murder, and mayhem stimuli of the crime scale, are not quantitatively defined. Where and how, by what rule, can these nonmetric stimuli be placed on the X axis to plot a function? Even the matching or numeric estimates to metric stimuli may be challenged. Assuming one uncovers a power function relationship, how much credence can be placed in the empirically obtained regression coefficient? How can we verify that judgments of the seriousness of crime are governed by a power function with a coefficient about .25? Why not, given a curvilinear relationship between magnitude and category scales of nonmetric stimuli, believe that the category scale is correct, the magnitude scale wrong, or both are wrong? To address these challenges directly, we must return to classical psychophysics, for the magnitude scaling and validation of social scales is dependent on the procedures developed for validating sensory scales.

3. THE VALIDATION OF MAGNITUDE SCALES

Early on in the development of magnitude scaling it was discovered that when subjects matched numbers to their impressions of different aspects of sight, sound, touch, smell, and taste, the empirically obtained power function exponent relating numeric estimation to each sensory modality varied reliably between one sensation and another. Different sensations grow at different, characteristic rates. Table 1 lists the characteristic power function exponents obtained by numeric estimation for a representative set of sensory continua under stringent laboratory controls. Since numeric estimation exhibits a unit (1.0) exponent, that is, people perceive numbers veridically, the exponents uncovered for each sensation were interpreted as a "signature" characterizing the impression of that specific sensation. So, for example, as shown in Table 1, when judged by numeric estimation, visual line length produces a characteristic exponent of 1.0, the brightness of a flash of light an exponent of .5, the exponents for sour, salty, and sweet tastes 1.3, 1.4, and .8, respectively. The exponent of 1.0 for line length means that the doubling of length will, typically, produce a doubling of the number response; the power function exponent of .67 for numeric estimates of loudness means that a doubling of decibels of sound pressure will characteristically produce the impression that the noise level is two-thirds louder; an exponent of 1.7 for force of hand grip means that when people estimate the strength of force exerted by squeezing a hand dynamometer, what appears to be a doubling of force is actually 3.3 times greater.

The range of sensations governed by the power law is impressive, covering aspects of all five senses, and equally impressive, the results of these psychophysical experiments are extremely reliable, typically reporting product-moment correlations of .99 between the magnitude of the stimuli and the geometric means of the numeric response.

These results, though impressive, were immediately challenged, critics rightfully arguing that the sole reliance on numeric estimation made it impossible to verify the power law, *or* confirm the characteristic exponent for each sensation, *or* prove the superiority of magnitude over category scales. Much like the perennial argument against verbal self-report response

TABLE 1

Representative Exponents of the Power Functions Relating Subjective Magnitude to Stimulus Magnitude

Continuum	Measured Exponent	Stimulus Condition
Loudness	0.67	Sound pressure of 3000-hertz tone
Vibration	0.95	Amplitude of 60 hertz on finger
Vibration	0.6	Amplitude of 250 hertz on finger
Brightness	0.33	5° Target in dark
Brightness	0.5	Point source
Brightness	0.5	Brief flash
Brightness	1.0	Point source briefly flashed
Lightness	1.2	Reflectance of gray papers
Visual length	1.0	Projected line
Visual area	0.7	Projected square
Redness (saturation)	1.7	Red-gray mixture
Taste	1.3	Sucrose
Taste	1.4	Salt
Taste	0.8	Saccharine
Smell	0.6	Heptane
Cold	1.0	Metal contact on arm
Warmth	1.6	Metal contact on arm
Warmth	1.3	Irradiation of skin, small area
Warmth	0.7	Irradiation of skin, large area
Discomfort, cold	1.7	Whole body irradiation
Discomfort, warm	0.7	Whole body irradiation
Thermal pain	1.0	Radiant heat on skin
Tactual roughness	1.5	Rubbing emery cloths
Tactual hardness	0.8	Squeezing rubber
Finger span	1.3	Thickness of blocks
Pressure on palm	1.1	Static force on skin
Muscle force	1.7	Static contractions
Heaviness	1.45	Lifted weights
Viscosity	0.42	Stirring silicone fluids
Vocal effort	1.1	Vocal sound pressure
Angular acceleration	1.4	5-Second rotation
Duration	1.1	White noise stimuli

Adapted from S. S. Stevens, 1975, reprinted by permission.

measures in the social sciences, psychophysicists objected to the reliance on such a "well-learned," "conscious," "judgmental" measure as numeric estimation, calling instead for some method to confirm the power law independent of numbers. The reply to each of these challenges—*cross-modality matching*—represents a significant contribution to the measurement of both sensory and social judgments.

The Cross-Modality Matching Paradigm

Matching is the basic operation of measurement, whether for measuring social or physical judgments. Some matching operations, of course, are more direct than others, just as some measures are better than others— their precision and accuracy verifiable by direct comparisons to a calibrated instrument or criterion. The cross-modality matching paradigm developed by J. C. Stevens et al. (1960) provides an elegant method for confirming the power law, for verifying the characteristic exponent relating stimulus magnitude to the magnitude of subjective response, and, by so soing, establishing *criteria* for the validation of sensory and social magnitude scales.

The logic and methods for dealing with the opposition to numeric estimation are simple and straightforward: *If* the coefficient for each sensation listed in Table 1 does in truth represent its characteristic exponent, then any one of these sensory modalities could in theory be used in lieu of numeric estimation as a magnitude response measure. Rather than have subjects match numbers to stimulus intensities, the experimenter could, for example, have subjects use force of hand grip or sound pressure as response modalities. So, to scale the brightness of light, each subject would be instructed to squeeze a calibrated hand dynamometer such that his impression of the force exerted by squeezing the hand grip matched his impression of the brightness of light: the brighter the light, the stronger the squeeze. Or, using sound pressure as a response modality, the subject would adjust a potentiometer to vary the loudness of sound in a pair of earphones such that the perceived loudness of noise matched his impression of the brightness of light: the brighter the light, the louder the noise. Sound difficult? In practice subjects oftentimes find these matching tasks easier than making numeric estimates and researchers often find that these physical response measures produce better fits to theory.

Figures 6 and 7 summarize the results of a series of studies matching force of hand grip and sound pressure, respectively, to a representative set of sensory variables. Of first concern is the relationship between sensations and the physical response measures. In each case the regression line drawn through the points by ordinary least squares provides a good fit to the data, with correlations in each case averaging .99. The plots relating the hand grip and loudness response measures to sensory continua are well-described by power functions. A basic conclusion drawn from these and similar plots using other response modalities is that the power law is not dependent on numeric estimation.

Given power function relationships relating force of hand grip and sound pressure to sensation, attention now focuses on the empirically

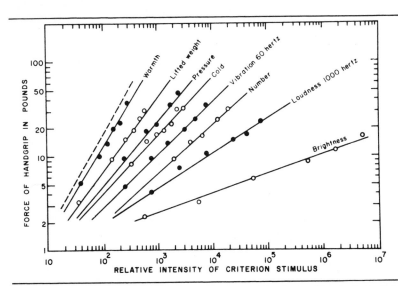

Figure 6: Equal sensation functions obtained by matching force of hand grip to various sensory continua. Each point stands for the median force exerted by 10 or more observers to match the apparent intensity of each stimulus. The dashed line shows a slope of 1.0 in these ratio-ruled coordinates. (From Stevens, 1966b; reprinted by permission.)

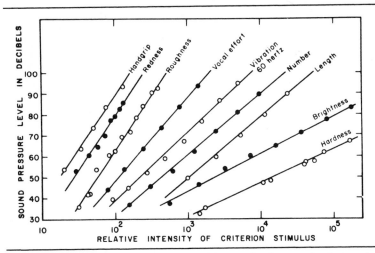

Figure 7: Equal sensation functions obtained by matches between loudness and various sensory continua. Each point represents the median sound pressure response averaged over 10 or more observers to each stimulus. (From Stevens, 1966b; reprinted by permission.)

obtained exponents. *If* the characteristic exponent for hand grip is indeed 1.7, as determined by numeric estimation, and that for loudness .67, *then* the slope for hand grip or loudness matches to any of the variables listed in Table 1 is, predictably, the ratio between the characteristic exponent of the stimulus and response variables. So, for example, in Figure 6, when force of hand grip responses are plotted as a function of brightness of light (.5), the predicted slope is $.5/1.7 = .29$, whereas, in Figure 7, when the same light stimuli are judged by sound pressure, the predicted slope is $.5/.67 = .75$. When the empirical exponents obtained by the hand grip and sound pressure matches to sensory variables are compared to the predicted power functions, the fit is remarkably close—on average, empirical exponents deviating less than 2% from the predicted ratios.

These results, replicated many times over, offer striking evidence in support of the characteristic exponents obtained by numeric estimation. What is more, by demonstrating that response modalities other than numbers can be used to build ratio scales, the way was cleared for the verification of scales by cross-modality matching.

The logic of the cross-modality matching paradigm is straightforward: If the power law is valid and if the exponents derived from magnitude estimation are truly characteristic, then any *two* quantitative response measures with established exponents could be used to judge a sensory continuum and the validity of the derived ratio scale confirmed by obtaining a close match between the theoretical and empirically obtained ratios *between the two response measures*. (Emphasis is used to alert the reader to a forthcoming solution to the practical question of what to plot on X in social scaling: One magnitude response measure on Y, the other magnitude response measure on X.)

The cross-modality matching paradigm requires the doubling up of the basic matching task: *Two* quantitative response modalities, each of which grows at a known, characteristic rate, are matched to each stimulus. The paradigm may be presented schematically as:

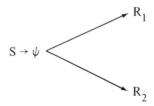

where S is the stimulus, say light, ψ (psi) the individual's *impression* of brightness, R_1 and R_2 the two quantitative response measures.[5]

The logic and methods of cross-modality matching are the same whatever the response measures (as long as they allow respondents to report relative magnitudes) and whatever the stimuli being scaled (as long as they are seen as attributes on a quantitative continuum). Let us first illustrate the paradigm using two physical response measures, loudness (sound pressure, SP) and force of hand grip (HG). To cross-modally validate a magnitude scale of apparent length, for example, subjects are instructed by appropriate changes in the prototypical instructions to adjust a knob attached to a potentiometer such that the loudness produced in a pair of earphones matches their impression of the apparent length of line: If a line seemed twice as long as the reference line, they would double their loudness respones, if half as long, halve the loudness. The matching procedure would then be repeated with force of hand grip as a response modality: The longer the line appeared to be, the stronger the squeeze; the shorter the line, the weaker the squeeze. The cross-modality matching paradigm establishes a simple analogy: My impression of this stimulus intensity (line) is to that stimulus intensity (line) as this loudness is to that loudness and this force of hand grip is to that force of hand grip. Because both magnitude response modalities are matched to the same set of stimuli, they are brought into a functional relationship on the principle of equivalence—objects equal to the same object are equal to each other.

In this example, since the characteristic exponent for sound pressure is .67 and that for force of hand grip is 1.7, when the sound pressure responses to each line length are logged, averaged, and their geometric means plotted in ratio-ruled coordinates against the corresponding hand grip responses, the result should be linear, a power function, with a slope equal to the characteristic ratio between the two response modalities, here $Sp^{.67}/HG^{1.7} = .39$. Within the cross-modality matching paradigm, a magnitude scale of impression is criterion validated when the empirical slope obtained from the matches to a common set of stimuli approximates the characteristic ratio between the two psychophysical response measures (Cross, 1974; Hamblin, 1974; Stevens, 1969, 1975).

Many such experiments investigating various modalities within the cross-modality matching paradigm establish the power law relationship governing the perception of most sensory continua and confirm their characteristic exponents. While any of the 30 sensory modalities listed in Table 1 could conceivably be used as quantitative response measures for scaling the perceived magnitude of stimuli, let us now illustrate the paradigm with two paper-and-pencil measures—*numeric estimation* (NE) and *line production* (LP, drawing lines to express the strength of one's impressions). To scale the brightness of lights, for example, the researcher would simply substitute "match numbers" and "draw lines" for "adjust loudness" and "squeeze hand grip" in the previous instructions. In this illustration, since the established exponent for numeric estimation is 1.0

and that for line drawing is also 1.0, when the geometric means obtained from matches to stimuli using these two response modalities are regressed one against the other on ratio-ruled coordinates, the result should be a power function with an empirical exponent equal to the established ratio between them of unity (1.0), since $NE^{1.0}/LP^{1.0} = 1.0$ (Stevens and Guirao, 1963; Teghtsoonian and Teghtsoonian, 1965). An important point: Do you see why the predicted ratio is a function of the two response modalities and not of the stimuli? It is because subjects are using the two responses to express their *impressions* of stimulus intensities.

Given the power of the cross-modality matching paradigm to verify ratio estimates of sensation, the question now before us is whether people can use these ratio scaling procedures to express the magnitude of their social-psychological impressions. If people can make only nominal or ordinal judgments on a dimension, then overspecifying the data as having interval or ratio properties will misrepresent the relations truly implied by their judgments. If, on the other hand, people are capable of making ratio judgments about the intensity of some social attributes, but only interval or ordinal judgments are recorded, the underspecificity will result in the loss of both information and proper access to powerful analytical tools. At issue here is the real and regrettable possibility that people may be capable of making ratio judgments of attributes on many social-psychological variables, but the data obtained by category scaling is merely ordinal or "quasi-interval."

The Transition from Sensory
to Social Psychophysical Scaling

The power law applies to those perceptual continua which vary in magnitude, where people are capable of judging "how much": How much stronger is my impression of this than that? Employing the cross-modality matching paradigm, the magnitude scaling of social-psychological impressions involves the simple substitution of social for physical stimuli: Typically, words and phrases denoting instances (items) on a social-psychological dimension stand in the place of the physical stimuli traditionally employed in classic psychophysics. The power of the cross-modality matching paradigm, and what especially recommends it for social scaling, is that the criterion test for validating a magnitude scale is primarily a function of the response modalities themselves, *not* the stimuli, on how close is the observed to predicted ratio between responses. The question, then, is: Do people perceive and respond to social stimuli as attributes of a quantitative variable? The answer can be determined empirically, for underlying the magnitude scaling of social-psychological variables is this criterion test: *The empirically obtained ratio between response modalities when matched to social stimuli should* approximate *the ratio established for the same two response modalities when matched to physical stimuli.* Emphasis is on "approximate" to signal the need for logical and statistical methods for comparing empirical to theoretical ratios.

There are, of course, statistically sound reasons to expect the empirical exponent to differ somewhat from the theoretical. Random influences alone will produce some departures from the norm. The characteristic exponent for each modality represents an average obtained in laboratory studies under rigorous experimental controls which eliminate or minimize such biases as order, range, and regression effects which perturb the characteristic exponent. While some of these second-order effects tend to steepen the empirical exponent and others make it more shallow, they do not always combine in such a way as to cancel one another out. This being the case, it is standard practice within sensory psychophysics to test for goodness of fit and accept as valid an empirical exponent which is included within the 95% confidence limits constructed around the theoretical exponent.

The same criteria can be applied to social scaling, but not as an absolute standard. Let reason prevail, for social scientists usually cannot exercise rigorous experimental controls in their studies and are consequently more at the whim of chance: Sometimes the confluence of biases combines to tilt the exponent off its characteristic axis. Because of these uncontrolled second-order effects, the 95% confidence limits around the theoretical exponent may on occasion exclude the empirical. One could of course simply relax the standard for survey research applications and accept as valid empirical exponents one additional step lower than the 95% confidence limits of the predicted. Given a power function relationship between response modalities and correlations between geometric means around .95+, the researcher would still be confident in the ratio properties of the scale.

A second alternative—this to be spelled out in ensuing sections—compares the empirical exponents obtained from the estimates of the social stimuli to the empirical exponents obtained from the same subjects when they match the same two response modalities to *metric* stimuli. Instead of making comparisons to the theoretical, one is directly comparing the social to metric exponents obtained from the *same* people within the *same* research setting. The assumption is that any biases affecting the responses to metric stimuli are working in the same direction and to much the same extent on the responses made to social stimuli. Here, the exponents empirically obtained from the matches to both metric and social stimuli are not expected to be statistically significant one from the other at the .05 level. This criterion test strikes us as a more reasonable standard for nonlaboratory applications of the cross-modality matching paradigm to social scaling.

Whichever criterion test an investigator employs to validate a magnitude scale of social judgments—whether one compares the empirically obtained regression coefficient to the theoretical slope, or to the slope derived from the matches made to the metric stimuli—it is important to keep in mind that the *basic* criterion is the same in both validity tests: Each of the empirical exponents and the ratio between them must be power functions. When this criterion is satisfied, the derived scale is rightfully labelled a psychophysically validated ratio scale.

The transition from sensory to social psychophysical scaling is not as great a leap as once assumed and no longer a barrier against the quantification of social judgments. This change in outlook came about in part from the realization that estimates of the intensity of physical stimuli are indeed judgments—*impressions* of the brightness of light, loudness of sound, heaviness of lifted weight—and in part as a consequence of successful applications of the cross-modality matching paradigm to social stimuli.

To the best of our knowledge, Dawson and Brinker's (1971) racism scale is the first published application of the cross-modality matching paradigm to social scaling. In their study, 24 undergraduates indicated their opinion of how much racism was implied by 13 descriptions of behavior by adjusting the loudness of a tone and squeezing a hand dynamometer. The items ranged from "A white student stated that he felt uneasy around black militants" to "A group of white men hanged and mutilated a Negro who was observed talking to a young white girl on the street." When the median force of hand grip was plotted against the median sound pressure response to each item on log-log coordinates, the function was linear, with a rank-order correlation of .97, and an empirically obtained slope of .38, which is a near perfect match to the predicted ratio of $SP^{.67}/HG^{1.7} = .39$, thereby confirming the internal validity of the racism scale.

An Adjectival Scale for Measuring Political Support

To illustrate the application of the cross-modality matching paradigm to social scaling, let us review a series of scaling studies carried out by Lodge and his associates (1975, 1976a, 1976b) to build and validate a scale measuring "support" for political institutions, policies, and leaders. This effort parallels explicitly the approach described earlier for the ratio scaling and cross-modal validation of sensory scales and had as one of its goals the extension of the cross-modality matching paradigm from laboratory to field research settings.

In contrast to most social-psychological scaling studies which include specific behavioral instances or attributes as scale items, for example, descriptions of racist acts, we opted to construct a scale made up of adjectival modifiers implying degrees of "approval-disapproval" which, we hoped, would be flexible and general enough to permit the ratio-level measurement of support for different leaders, policies, and institutions in survey instruments.

From a pool of 160 words and phrases used in everyday language and existing social science category scales, a set of 30 adjectives and adjectival phrases, among them "excellent," "very good," "good," "so-so," "bad," "very bad," and "terrible," were selected as scale items. To determine whether these adjectival modifiers convey quantitative information, and if so their generalizability as expressions of approval-disapproval for different political objects, a series of magnitude scaling experiments were carried out, beginning with student subjects in the laboratory and then moving out into "real world" in local field studies and finally into a national survey. Let us briefly summarize the experimental studies employing physical response measures within the cross-modality matching paradigm and then concentrate on the study employing paper-and-pencil measures in a survey.

A Laboratory-Derived Scale of Support. Subjects were 48 college students who participated in the first laboratory study using numeric estimation, force of hand grip, and sound pressure as response modalities to estimate the amount of support conveyed by the 30 adjectival descriptors. To provide a context for the evaluation of items, each of the modifiers was embedded in one or more simple declarative statements: "The U.S. Senate is . . ."; "The local Suffolk County Police is . . ."; "The Supreme Court's decision on abortion is . . ."; and (then-) "President Nixon's handling of domestic affairs is . . . ." There were 13 adjectival descriptors which made up each scale, and all judgments were made relative to the reference item (" . . . so-so"), which was assigned 50 units of support for NE and a "comfortable" squeeze and noise level for the HG and SP responses. Of the subjects, 16 scaled the items in the Senate, Police, and Court decision scales, and all 48 subjects scaled the items in the Nixon scale. Note that subjects are scaling the amount of support expressed by items, *not* how much they agree or disagree with the statement. If the adjectival descriptors can be shown to represent quantitatively meaningful values, subjects could later be asked to choose the item which best expresses their opinion of the Senate, Court decision, police, or Nixon, and

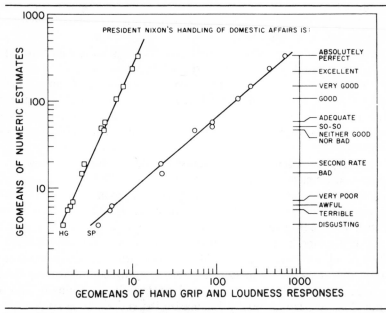

Figure 8: Numeric estimates are plotted on ratio-ruled coordinates as a function of force of hand grip (HG) and loudness (SP) responses to 13 adjectival scale items implying degrees of approval-disapproval for President Nixon's handling of domestic affairs. Each point is the geometric mean pooled over 48 subjects. (From Lodge et al., 1975; reprinted by permission.)

the investigator then assign magnitude rather than categorical weights to their opinions.

The scaling experiment proceeded in stages. First, to give subjects practice in making magnitude judgments, they matched NE, HG, and SP to a sequence of line lengths. Upon completion of this training exercise, they were instructed to use the same three response modalities to estimate the amount of support implied by each statement compared to the reference item " . . . so-so."

The geometric means of the numeric estimation responses to the 13 adjectival descriptors embedded in the Nixon scale are plotted on log-log coordinates as a function of the geometric means of the hand grip and loudness responses in Figure 8. The data points have been displaced along the X-axis to achieve clarity in the display. Each point represents the geometric mean pooled over 48 subjects to each item for each of the two physical response modalities separately. As is clear from visual inspection of the plots, the best fitting lines drawn through the HG and SP response data are well-described by power functions. Plots for the adjectival descriptors in the Senate, Police, and Court scales look and behave similarly (Lodge et al., 1975).

Lacking known metric properties for the social stimuli against which to regress the magnitude judgments of support, the cross-modality matching paradigm calls for comparisons between the response modalities. The product-moment correlation between the geometric means relating NE and HG is .998, for NE and SP, .981, and between the two physical response measures, HG and SP, .99. These correlation coefficients indicate a high degree of linear dependence between log response measures which, of course, is precisely what the underlying psychophysical theory predicts because of the functional relations presumed to hold among these response variables. These correlations indicate residual variances of only .4%, 3.8%, and 2% unexplained by the linear regressions in log-log coordinates.

The fit of the linear regression equation to each of the three response modalities is good in each case—a power function—implying that these subjects were using these continuous response measures to make ratio judgments of the scale items in terms of support. Each of the regression slopes, however, differs from the theoretical, a consequence of our inability to adequately control for such second-order effects as the presentation order of stimuli, the proclivity of people to round off numbers when making numeric estimates, and their tendency to attenuate responses. The empirical exponents obtained from the matches to the line length stimuli used in the practice task *and* to the social stimuli are excluded from the 95% confidence limits of the theoretic, but do satisfy the less stringent criterion test for social judgments.

To better understand the criterion test for validating social scales, let us look more closely at the response data relating the two physical modalities to both the metric and social stimuli. First, compare the exponents and ratios obtained from the HG and SP matches made by these subjects to *line length* stimuli:

The criterion is:	$SP^{.67}/HG^{1.7} = .39$
For the 16 subjects in the Senate scale:	$SP^{.54}/HG^{1.3} = .42$
For the 16 subjects in the Police scale:	$SP^{.58}/HG^{1.4} = .41$
For the 16 subjects in the Court scale:	$SP^{.57}/HG^{1.6} = .36$
For the 48 subjects in the Nixon scale:	$SP^{.56}/HG^{1.3} = .43.$

Each of the empirical regression exponents is lower than the predicted slopes of .67 and 1.7. This is a classic instance of regression bias: The respondents tended to slightly overestimate the intensity of weak stimuli and underestimate the strength of strong stimuli. The result of regression bias is to tilt the regression exponent downward from its theoretical slope. As a response bias common to all human judgmental processes, it is usually the case, as here, to find that the direction and extent of regression bias operating on the magnitude response measures affects each of them more or less similarly. In the matches made to the line length stimuli, the confluence of biases affects both the SP and HG responses symmetrically—on average the SP responses are tilted 4.6 degrees lower and the HG responses 5.3 degrees lower than the predicted exponents. Note that because the regression effects are symmetrical, the SP/HG ratio obtained from each group of subjects is a close match to the predicted ratio of .39.

Now compare the exponents and ratios obtained from the same subjects using the same response modalities to estimate the amount of approval-disapproval expressed by the adjectival modifiers embedded in the four *social scales*:

The criterion is:	$SP^{.67}/HG^{1.7} = .39$
The Senate scale is:	$SP^{.57}/HG^{1.3} = .44$
The Police scale is:	$SP^{.64}/HG^{1.5} = .43$
The Court scale is:	$SP^{.56}/HG^{1.6} = .35$
The Nixon scale is:	$SP^{.55}/HG^{1.4} = .40.$

Once again, although the empirical exponents differ from the theoretical, the direction and extent of regression bias on both the HG and SP responses are similar: On average the SP exponents are tilted 3.6 degrees lower and the HG exponents 4.3 degrees lower than the theoretically expected. Here, too, as was the case for the matches made to the metric stimuli, the direction and extent of bias operating on both magnitude response measures are similar, so the critical SP/HG ratio test for each social scale includes the empirical .39 exponent within the 95% confidence limits of the theoretical. What is particularly noteworthy is the close match of exponents and ratios between responses obtained from these subjects to both the social and metric variables under these research conditions: The second-order effects operate on *both* responses to both the metric *and* social stimuli similarly. This being the case, our inability to retrieve the theoretical exponents is seen as a simple result of our inability to adequately control the biases operating on the response measures within this specific research setting, not as a failure of the subjects to make ratio judgments of the adjectival modifiers in terms of approval-disapproval.

In later sections we provide a simple method to correct for regression bias. At this point it is important to recognize that when, as here, the response measures are highly correlated and well-described as power functions, the empirically obtained scale, whether biased or not, is a power function of the theoretical scale. To wit: If social scale values for each stimulus on the Nixon scale were calculated from the empirical slope of .40 ($SP^{.55}/HG^{1.4}$) and plotted against scale values calculated from the theoretical slope of .39, the two scales would be linearly related in log-log coordinates. The difference in slope between .39 and .40 represents the degree of departure from the "true" scale.

The empirically obtained scale values for the 30 adjectival descriptors are summarized in Table 2. The first four column headings indicate the context (Senate, Police, Court decision, Nixon) within which subjects estimated the support implied by each modifier. The scale value (fifth column) for each of the 30 modifiers is the geometric mean averaged over the NE, HG, and SP estimates of support for all subjects. The magnitude range of this adjectival scale is 98:1, from "Absolutely perfect" (ψ = 332) to "Disgusting" (ψ = 3.4).

Of the 30 adjectival phrases used in this study, 16 appear in two or more scales. Despite differences in the linguistic content of the scales and differences in context, some startling invariances appear in the quantitative relations among adjectives. The description "absolutely perfect," for example, is 6.9 times more favorable than "so-so" on the Senate scale and 6.6 times more favorable on the Nixon scale. On the police scale "mediocre" expresses 70% of the support expressed by "so-so," and on the Court scale it is 68%. The description "good" appears on all four scales. Its magnitude relative to "so-so" for each is 2.1, 2.4, 2.0, and 2.1. On average, "good" is about two times more favorable than the reference "so-so."

An additional source of invariance can be found in the effect of the modifier *very* on a descriptor word. When modifying the words *good, bad,* or *poor,* the magnitude of the increase or decrease in the word's scale value relative to "so-so" is approximately the same. On the Nixon scale, "very good" is 1.4 times more supportive than "good"; "very bad" on the Senate scale is 1.4 times worse than "bad"; "very poor" on the Police scale is 1.4 times worse than "poor"; and on the Senate scale "very good" is 1.2 times more supportive than "good." At this point, the reader may find it helpful to compare the scale values, relative to "so-so," for some of the more popular adjectives used to anchor category scales or designate the range

TABLE 2
Strength of Support Expressed by Thirty Adjective
Phrases: Comparison Across Scales

Scale Item	Senate	Police	Court Decision	Nixon's Policy	Geometric Mean
Absolutely perfect	343			328	332
Perfect		286	307		296
Excellent		237		232	233
Great		217			217
Terrific	207				207
First rate			200		200
Very good	126			146	141
Good	106	121	100	105	107
Satisfactory		77	66		71
Adequate	43			57	53
Sometimes all right		51			51
So-so	(50)	(50)	(50)	(50)	(50)
Good and bad	47				47
Neither good nor bad			47	46	46
Mediocre		35	34		34
Inadequate	29				29
Not so good		21			21
Below par			20		20
Second rate			20	19	19
Bad	16			15	15
Unsatisfactory	15		10		12
Very bad	12				12
Poor		10			10
Very poor		7		7	7
Third rate			8		7
Terrible	6	8		6	6
Dreadful		6			6
Awful			5	6	6
Atrocious	4				4
Disgusting			3	4	3

Adapted from Lodge, Cross, Tursky and Tanehaus, 1975, reprinted by permission.

and dimension of popular social science scales. Compare, for example, such pairs as: good versus bad, very good versus very bad, adequate versus inadequate, excellent versus terrible, and first rate versus second rate. In no case are the polar adjectives equally distant from the standard "so-so." Note, too, that the most popular polar adjectives provide a narrow range.

A summary measure of the reliability of the magnitude values across scales is the .99 product-moment correlation for the 16 repeated words between each word's strength on one scale and its strength on another. In general, the pattern of invariances found here suggests that these scales are highly reliable and valid indicators of strength of support.

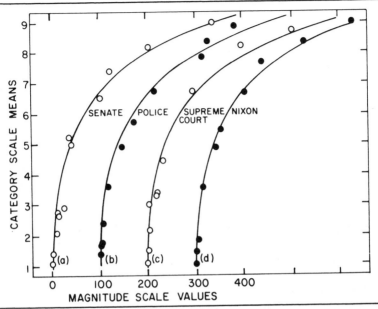

Figure 9: Comparison between categorical and magnitude judgments of the amount of approval-disapproval implied by adjectival scale items embedded in each scale: (a) the U.S. Senate, (b) local police, (c) Supreme Court decision on abortion, and (d) Nixon's handling of his job as President. Magnitude scale values averaged across geometric means of the NE, HG, and SP responses have been displaced along the ratio-ruled X-axis for clarity.

Equally predictable is the relationship between magnitude and categorical measures of support. At the conclusion of this study, subjects were asked to rate the amount of approval-disapproval expressed by each statement on a 9-point category scale labelled "Strong Approval" at one end and "Strong Disapproval" at the other. In Figure 9 the mean category ratings are plotted as a function of the magnitude scale values on semilog coordinates for each of the four scales. The relationship between scales is, predictably, markedly nonlinear.[6]

Testing the Support Scale in the Real World. These laboratory results indicate that some of the adjectival modifiers of support convey more precise information about the relative magnitude of opinion strength than heretofore expected. But the possibility remains that these apparent invariances are peculiar to the linguistic behavior of college students in a laboratory setting. Before the scale items could be tested in a survey setting, two questions need be addressed: First, could "real world" people make proportional judgments of the support implied by these words and phrases? And, equally important, would the metric relations between the adjectival modifiers of support found for students hold for adults outside the laboratory?

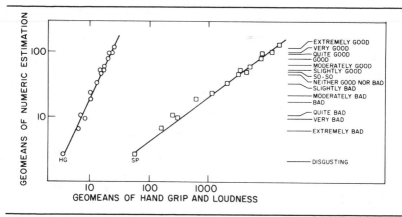

Figure 10: Numeric estimates are plotted as a function of force of hand grip (HG) and loudness (SP) responses on ratio-ruled coordinates for 15 adjectival descriptors of support for the U.S. Supreme Court's decision on abortion. Each point is the geometric mean averaged over the 111 Long Island, New York, respondents of the Lodge et al. (1976) survey (reprinted by permission).

For this validation experiment—administered in the individual's home using portable equipment with the capability of delivering line length and word stimuli and eliciting NE, HG, and SP responses—111 of 123 local area adults completed the metric and social scaling tasks. Each subject first made NE, HG, and SP estimates of a sequence of line lengths, then used the three response modalities to estimate the amount of support implied by 26 of the adjectival modifiers from the laboratory study. Once again the scale items were embedded in simple declarative sentences ("The Supreme Court's decision on abortion is . . ." or "The Democratic Party is . . . ,") with all magnitude judgments made relative to the reference " . . . so-so."

The results of this study are reported in detail in Lodge et al. (1976a). Synoptically, despite mechanical problems related to the potentiometer used for making loudness judgments, these adult subjects reveal an ability to make proportional judgments of the relative intensity of both metric and social stimuli. Figure 10 displays the NE responses plotted as a function of the SP and HG matches to the adjectival modifiers of support embedded in the Court scale. The plot of the geometric means in each case approximates the expected ratio relationship between modalities.

Scales derived from each of three response modalities are in close agreement: The intercorrelations between the NE, HG, and SP modalities for the Party Support scale are .98, .93, and .91 and for the Court scale, .98, .97, and .98. The high intercorrelations between responses indicate an underlying psychological continuum corresponding to strength of support, while the close fit between obtained and predicted regression exponents provides strong evidence of the psychophysical validity of the scale.

To test the generalizability of the Support scale, the scale values derived from the NE, HG, and SP matches of this adult sample were plotted against the scale values obtained from undergraduates in the laboratory study for the 26 words common to both samples. The correlation between the two sets of scale values is .995, with a regression coefficient in log-log coordinates of .94, which is included within the 95% confidence limits of the theoretic. These results suggests a good deal of consensus among people as to the information conveyed by these adjectival modifiers of support.

The key point to be made in concluding this overview of cross-modality matching is that the paradigm generates all the information required to determine the scalability of variables and, what is more, constitutes a stringent test for confirming or disconfirming the internal validity of scales. Not only must the empirically derived relationships between response modalities result in a power function but, still more exacting, the empirical exponent obtained from the matches to social stimuli must approximate the established ratio between exponents or, when bias is present, approximate the empirical exponents obtained from the matches to the physical stimuli used in the practice task. When either criterion is met, the derived scale is psychophysically valid. If, on the other hand, subjects are not using the response modalities properly to make proportional judgments, the empirically obtained relationship between response modalities will not be a power function. Nor will the criterion validity test be satisfied if the scale items are not consensually perceived as attributes of a quantitative continuum.

At this juncture—given the apparent power to build and validate magnitude scales of social opinion—Tanenhaus and Murphy elected to employ the cross-modality matching paradigm in a national survey carried out in 1974 by the University of Michigan's Survey Research Center to measure support for the U.S. Supreme Court and its decisions (see Lodge et al., 1976b; Tanenhaus and Murphy, 1981). Because of the heavy reliance on interview and survey research in the social and behavioral sciences, let us detail the methods employed in this study for building and cross-modally validating scales of social opinion and, in passing, address general problems of magnitude scaling raised in the earlier introductory sections.

4. THE MAGNITUDE SCALING AND VALIDATION
OF SOCIAL OPINION SCALES IN SURVEY RESEARCH

The logic and methods for social psychophysical scaling parallel explicitly the cross-modality matching methodology established for the magnitude scaling of sensory variables. Procedurally, words and phrases denoting attributes or instances on a social-psychological dimension (as, for example, the adjectival modifiers of support) are substituted for the physical stimuli used in sensory psychophysics. The collection of response data, analyses, computation of magnitude scale values, plots, and validation tests are the same whether the stimuli being judged are lines, numbers, lights, sounds, or words and phrases denoting social-psychological attributes. Social scaling can be (we argue "should be") procedurally identical. The methods and procedures proposed here represent a concerted effort to establish a logical and methodological isomorphism between social and sensory scaling. The closer the parallel, the stronger the criterion test for cross-modal validation of the social-psychological scale.

General Procedures for Survey Research Applications

Our adaptation of the cross-modality matching paradigm to survey research involves subjects in two scaling tasks. The first task is the "calibration" task, in which subjects are given instruction and practice in the use of two quantitative response modalities to make proportional judgments of *metric* stimuli. This procedure serves three functions: First and foremost it is a vehicle for instruction in making magnitude judgments. Without instruction, some subjects would make ordinal judgments. Second, the advantage of having subjects use the two response modalities in matches to metric stimuli is that analyses of these response data allow the researcher to determine whether the subjects are making proportional judgments, and if so how accurately. And last, the functions obtained from the matches to the metric stimuli can be used to estimate the effects of bias operating on the response modalities and under some conditions correct for it.

The second task is the actual social scaling task, in which subjects use the same two response modalities to judge the perceived intensity of social scale items on a social-psychological dimension.

Response Modalities. While any of the sensory variables listed in Table 1 could conceivably be used as continuous response measures in field research, cost and technical considerations preclude most psychophysical measures. Several criteria govern the choice of response measures for survey applications. The modalities must: (1) have well-established exponents, (2) provide a response range on the order of 100:1 which is oftentimes uncovered in social scales, (3) be portable and inexpensive, (4) be capable of administration by interviewers untutored in psychophysics, and (5) be easily embedded in a more or less conventional interview schedule.

The obvious first choice for one response modality is *numeric estimation.* As the most widely used response measure in both sensory and social psychophysical scaling, NE exhibits a stable exponent of 1.0 across wide ranges of stimuli.

Of the other continuous response measures available, *Line Production* (LP, drawing lines to express the strength of one's impressions) best satisfies the criteria for survey research. Line Production is a well-documented psychophysical modality which, like numeric estimation, has a characteristic exponent of 1.0 (Stevens and Guirao, 1963; Teghtsoonian and Teghtsoonian, 1965). As a paper-and-pencil measure, LP, like NE, is linear within the 100:1 range, portable, inexpensive to administer, record, and score, and relatively easy to incorporate into a standard interview instrument. The one drawback of the line-drawing response is its tendency, more so than NE, to be regressive—people tend to draw lines a bit longer than they should to weak stimuli and shorter than called for to strong stimuli—the result being that the empirical exponent is typically somewhat lower than the characteristic slope of unity.

The Survey Instrument. Given line drawing as a response modality, a number of laboratory and field tests were conducted to determine the characteristics of LP under survey conditions using different survey formats (Lodge et al., 1976b). The physical dimensions of the survey instrument should provide adequate length for a subject to draw lines without constraint. Ideally, the subject should have an unconstrained response range to work with, perhaps an infinitely long strip of paper for drawing lines, just as in numeric estimation there is theoretically no upper bound to the numbers an individual can use. Practically speaking, if the objective range of the metric stimuli or subjective range of the social stimuli exceeds the available range of the response, the magnitude judgments will be attenuated.

Rather than describe the results of various tests of different line-drawing procedures and survey formats, let it suffice to report the compromise. The survey instrument put in the field by Michigan's Survey Research Center was printed lengthwise on legal-size (8.5″ × 14″) paper. Within this practical limit, the typical survey respondent can make relatively unconstrained LP judgments in excess of the 100:1 range set as a minimum. All the research reported here using line-drawing responses was made within this survey format.[7]

The Calibration of Response Modalities

The calibration procedure—a 6- to 8-minute prelude to social scaling—is a straightforward psychophysical scaling task which provides subjects with the training and practice required to use the two response modalities to make proportional judgments. Employing numeric estimation and line drawing—the same two response modalities the respondents will later use to judge the intensity of social stimuli—the simplest, most direct approach for the calibration of responses is to have subjects make numeric estimates of line length stimuli (e.g., lines 3 mm, 6 mm, 20 mm, 35 mm, 100 mm, 150 mm, 225 mm, and 300 mm in length, relative to a 50 mm line) and then draw lines to a series of number stimuli of equal value (i.e., the numbers 3, 6, 20, 35, 100, 150, 225, and 300, relative to the number 50). Nine to 12 metric stimuli covering a 100:1 range should suffice to produce the desired effect of introducing subjects to the idea of magnitude scaling and provide the investigator with sufficient information to evaluate their performance.

Instructions for the Calibration of the Line and Number Response Measures. Many psychophysical scaling studies report verbatim the instructions used. (See Stevens, 1975, for their development and increasing simplicity; Hamblin, 1974: 63-65, for "rules of thumb"; Coleman and Rainwater, 1978: Appendix B, for clever variations.) The Tanenhaus-Murphy CPS/SRC instructions for the calibration of response measures read:

> This booklet contains a series of line lengths. Please leaf through the booklet and notice that some of the lines are longer than the first line and some of the lines are shorter than the first line. Your task is to tell how much longer or shorter they are compared to the first line. The first line is your reference. We have given it the number 50.
>
> [50]
>
> The number 50 is your reference. All you need do is write a number in the box for each line. The longer a line appears to be compared to your reference line, the bigger the number you will write in compared to 50. For example, if one of the lines seems about two times longer than the reference line, you would write in the number 100. If a line were ten times longer, you would write in the number 500. On the other hand, some of the lines are shorter than the reference. If a line were about one half as long, you would write in a number

about one half of 50, about 25. Another line about one tenth as long would be given the number one tenth of 50, 5. Give each line a number, whatever number seems appropriate, to express how the line compares to your reference line: The longer the line, the bigger your number compared to 50. The shorter the line, the smaller your number compared to 50. Once you begin, please do not turn back to check your numbers or look at the reference line. We are only interested in your general impressions.

Immediately after making numeric estimates of the line length stimuli, subjects were handed a second booklet, this containing the number stimuli, one per page in irregular order, and directed by appropriate changes in the instructions to draw lines relative to a 50 mm line assigned the number 50.

50

The larger the number compared to 50, the longer their line-drawing response compared to the reference line; the smaller the number compared to 50, the shorter the line they would draw.

The instructions and matching exercises are designed to provide respondents with the practical training and conceptual wherewithal to use the response modalities to make proportional judgments which are flexible enough to track stimuli across a wide range and sensitive enough to discriminate small changes in stimulation. Given proper instruction the majority of subjects grasp the idea of proportionality quickly, others more slowly, and some poor souls, between 3% and 5%, for physical or psychological reasons, never do.

The second rationale for the calibration procedure is a "concession" to the lack of known, objectively measurable values for social stimuli. Because the value of each number and line length stimulus is known and presented without error, an investigator can determine whether the respondents are using the response modalities properly to make proportional judgments by simply regressing the geometric means of their numeric estimates of the line length stimuli agains the actual millimeters of line length (as you did in Exercise A) and regressing the geometric means of their line-drawing responses against the actual values of the number stimuli. If, in a given study, a social magnitude scale were to fail, analyses of these calibration data answer the question: "Did subjects understand and use the two response measures properly to make proportional judgments?" If their numeric estimates and line-drawing responses are found to be a power function of the metric stimuli, then any problem with the social scale must be assumed to lie with the social stimuli and/or social-psychological dimension. If, on the other hand, the calibration data fail to meet the criterion test, the fault lies in the magnitude scaling instructions or the subjects, most probably the instructions.

The third rationale for this formal practice task, and what leads us to call it "calibration" rather than "practice," harks to the earlier discussion of cross-modal validation. Because both the numeric estimation and line production response measures grow at a characteristic rate, each of the empirical exponents derived from the matches to the metric stimuli will result in a power function with a slope close to 1.0 *if* the respondents are in fact using the response modalities to make unbiased proportional judgments. The empirical exponents and NE/LP ratio obtained from the matches to the metric stimuli can therefore be used to estimate the direction and extent of bias operating on the response modalities within the particular research setting and, if bias is present, be used to evaluate the exponents obtained from the matches made to the social stimuli and under most conditions correct for regression bias.

Preparation of Calibration Data. The NE matches to line length stimuli and LP matches to numbers is a straightforward cross-modality matching task, and the analysis of response data is standardized. The steps are those spelled out in Exercise A except, of course the LP responses must first be measured by a ruler (in millimeters).[8] After separately tallying the NE and LP responses to each stimulus, one takes the common log of each response, calculates the arithmetic mean of the logs, and then exponentiates the mean of the logs to obtain the geometric mean.

Casual inspection of magnitude response data in this tabular form often reveals a number of characteristics of the NE and LP response modalities. For instance, subjects typically round off their numeric estimates: Few subjects use odd numbers; most favor multiples of 5 and 10. A small percentage of subjects will make numeric estimates which are uninterpretable, for example, NE responses of zero, or at the other extreme, 10^{10}. These responses are treated as missing data. Though not evident in matches made to metric stimuli, one sometimes finds that some responses to social stimuli are exceedingly high compared to the general consensus. Taking the logs of magnitude responses pulls these outliers toward the center. In general the distribution of responses is skewed more to the right than assumed by arithmetically normal distribution, so the arithmetic mean is not a good measure of central tendency for these response distributions.

Calculation of the Geometric Mean

The median or, more usefully, the geometric mean is the standard measure of central tendency with magnitude data. It is, in effect, the ordinary mean computed on variables that have been transformed into logs. The general formula for the geometric mean (Blalock, 1964) is:

$$\text{Geomean} = \sqrt[n]{x_1, x_2, x_3 \ldots x_n},$$

which is simply the antilog of the mean of the logarithms and is calculated directly by exponentiating the arithmetic mean of the logs.[9] The geometric mean assumes that the distribution of magnitude responses is log-normal but is little affected by the steep peakedness (leptokurtosis) characteristic of the distribution of magnitude response data.

To compute the variance around the geometric mean, first calculate the standard deviation about the arithmetic mean of the responses in the usual way for each stimulus and then multiply the standard deviation by the ratio of the geometric to arithmetic mean to obtain a "corrected" standard deviation of the geometric mean. As Shinn (1974: 139-141) notes, this procedure smoothes somewhat the relationship between the means and standard deviations, but the difference between "corrected" and ordinary standard deviations is not marked. Most researchers simply use the standard deviation.

Analysis of the Cross-Modal Matches to the Calibrating Metric

Making numeric estimates of line length stimuli and drawing lines to number stimuli is a straightforward psychophysical scaling task which can be analyzed directly by regressing the geometric means of each magnitude response against the respective values of the calibrating stimuli on log-log coordinates. Figure 2, presented earlier in the introduction to illustrate the basic magnitude scaling approach, displays the results for the numeric estimates of line length stimuli obtained from the 375 subjects in the Tanenhaus-Murphy survey. The empirical relationship is linear on log-log coordinates, with a Pearson product-moment correlation of .995 relating the geometric means of NE to the metric stimuli, and an ordinary least squares regression coefficient of .988. This close power function fit of empirical to predicted exponent demonstrates that these survey responents are using the NE response modality to make unconstrained proportional judgments.

The LP matches to the number stimuli for the 375 subjects in the Michigan survey are plotted in Figure 11. The relationship is also linear on log-log coordinates and highly correlated at .99, indicating that these subjects are drawing lines proportional to the metric stimuli. But, as is obvious by visual inspection of the plot, the empirically obtained regres-

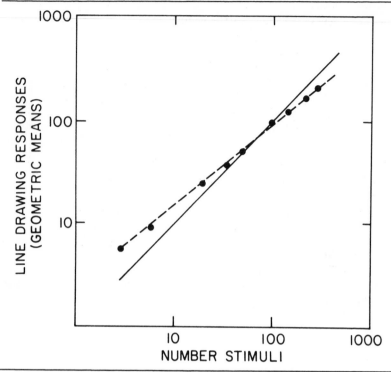

Figure 11: Line-drawing responses plotted as a function of nine number stimuli on logarithmic coordinates. Each point represents the geometric mean of the line-drawing response averaged over 375 respondents in the Murphy-Tanenhaus national sample. The solid line drawn through the plot represents the theoretical exponent of 1.0, and the dashed line drawn through the points is the empirically obtained exponent of .802.

sion coefficient of .802 (dashed line) is lower than the predicted unit exponent and excluded from the 95% confidence limits constructed around the theoretical slope (solid line). This is neither an uncommon nor surprising result, since LP is oftentimes found to be regressive and will warrant the application of a correction factor when computing social scale values if, as expected, the same regressive tendency is found for the LP matches to the social stimuli.

Another way of analyzing the calibration data—this explicitly analogous to the analysis of social stimuli—is to regress the geomeans of one response modality against the geomeans of the other response modality on log-log coordinates. This cross-modality comparison is made possible by having both sets of calibrating stimuli—the line lengths and numbers—of equal value. The criterion test for verifying this indirect cross-modal

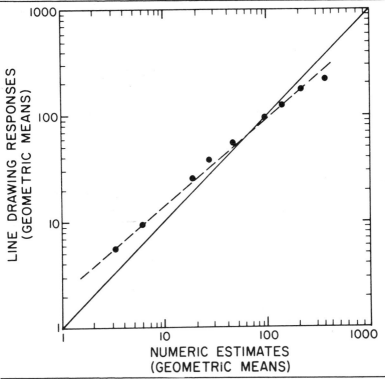

Figure 12: Line-drawing responses are plotted as a function of numeric estimates to a common set of nine metric stimuli. Each point on the graph is the geometric mean averaged over 375 respondents in the Murphy-Tanenhaus national sample. The solid line is the predicted exponent of 1.0, the dashed line the obtained exponent of .879.

relationship is of course the same as that established for the validation of responses when matched directly against the metric stimuli: The empirical NE/LP ratio should be included within the 95% confidence limits constructed around the theoretical ratio of $(NE^{1.0}/LP^{1.0} =)$ 1.0.

Figure 12 displays this cross-modal match between the geometric means of the NE and LP response measures. The relationship between responses in log-log coordinates is linear, a power function, as predicted by psychophysical theory and as expected given each response modality's linear performance in Figures 2 and 11 when matched against the *metric stimuli*. The correlation between response modalities is strong, .989, and the empirical exponent of .879 (dashed line) is, as expected, lower than the theoretic because LP is regressive.[10]

Error-in-Both-Variables Regression

Note that in contrast to the plots in Figures 2 and 11 which relate each response modality directly against the metric stimuli, the plot in Figure 12 represents the *indirect* cross-modality matching paradigm: Both measures on both axes are responses, in effect, dependent variables. The independent variable is the stimuli eliciting both responses. Because the two responses are made with some error, ordinary least squares is not appropriate. Rather, an *error-in-both-variables* regression model is used to estimate parameters:

$$\beta = \sqrt{\Sigma Y^2 - \frac{(\Sigma Y)^2}{n}} \Bigg/ \sqrt{\Sigma X^2 - \frac{(\Sigma X)^2}{n}}$$

Or, more simply:

$$\beta = S_y/S_x,$$

when the response measures are in logarithms (Cross, 1974).[11]

This *indirect* cross-modality matching paradigm employing error-in-both-variables regression is identical to the model used for analyzing social stimuli: Two response measures are brought into a functional relationship by being matched to a common set of stimuli.

Survey Instructions for the Magnitude Scaling of Social Items

Immediately following the calibration task, each subject was handed another booklet and instructed in the use of numeric estimation and line drawing to judge the amount of approval-disapproval implied by 13 items from the original support scale. The social-scaling instructions essentially substitute "words and phrases expressing different amounts of approval or disapproval" for "lines" and "numbers" in the calibrating instructions, "more approval" and "less approval" for "longer" and "shorter" line lengths, and "larger" and "smaller" numbers. The core instructions read:

Now that you have practiced using numbers and drawing lines, we are going to ask you to give numbers and draw lines to words like these on this practice page. (Hand subject 8.5" × 14" sheet containing 6 words printed lengthwise: SO-SO, EXCELLENT, GOOD, BAD, PERFECT, DISGUSTING.) We want you to use numbers to say how much approval or disapproval these words express as compared to the reference word "SO-SO." "SO-SO" is your reference word. We have given it the number 50.

So-So
[50]

Note that some of the words on this page express more approval than SO-SO, and others express less approval than SO-SO. The greater the amount of approval a word expresses compared to SO-SO, the bigger the number you write in compared to 50. The less the amount of approval a word expresses, the smaller the number you write in compared to 50 for SO-SO. For example, if you think one of the words expresses about two times more approval than SO-SO, you would write in the number 100. If a word expressed ten times more approval than SO-SO, you would write in the number 500. On the other hand, if a word expresses less approval than SO-SO, you would write in a number lower than 50. A word expressing half the approval of SO-SO would get the number 25. A word expressing one tenth the amount of approval would get the number one tenth of 50, that is, 5.

Let's take some examples. If someone said a TV program was "SO-SO," we would give SO-SO the number 50. Now suppose someone else said it was EXCELLENT. The word EXCELLENT expresses more approval than the word SO-SO. How much more? If you think it expresses much more approval, you write in a number much bigger than 50. If you think it expresses only a little more approval than SO-SO, you write in a number only a little bigger than 50. There is no exact number. Everyone thinks of words differently and uses numbers differently, so you should write in any number compared to 50 that seems right to you. (Subject writes in number for EXCELLENT.)

Now, suppose someone said that something was GOOD. If you think the word GOOD expresses more approval than SO-SO, you would give it a number larger than 50. What number would you give GOOD? (Subject writes in number on practice sheet. Any number larger than 50 is acceptable. If response is ≤50, interviewer repeats paragraph 2.)

Suppose someone said something was BAD. If you think the word BAD expresses less approval than SO-SO, you would write in a number smaller than .50. Write in a number for BAD compared to 50. (Any number less than 50 is acceptable. If number is ≥50, interviewer repeats paragaph 2.)

OK. Let's try PERFECT. Relative to your reference number 50 for SO-SO, what number would you give to PERFECT?

The last word is DISGUSTING. Compared to SO-SO, what number would you give DISGUSTING?

Upon completion of this practice exercise:

Here is a booklet (8.5″ × 14″, containing 13 words printed lengthwise one per page, in irregular order, with SO-SO appearing first: SO-SO, ABSOLUTELY PERFECT, EXCELLENT, TERRIFIC, VERY

GOOD, GOOD, SATISFACTORY, NOT ADEQUATE, NOT SO GOOD, BAD, VERY BAD, TERRIBLE, DISGUSTING). Please flip through the pages and note that some of the words express more approval than SO-SO, some words express less approval, and some of the words are near the middle. Please write a number on each page compared to 50 to show how much or how little approval each word expresses compared to the reference word SO-SO. Once you begin, please don't turn back to any of your other numbers. We are interested in your general impression.

Immediately following the matching of numbers to the amount of approval-disapproval implied by each of the 13 scale items, subjects were instructed by appropriate changes in these instructions to draw lines to words relative to a 50 mm line assigned the reference item "so-so."

Of the 404 respondents interviewed in the Tanenhaus-Murphy survey, 375 successfully carried out the calibration and social scaling tasks. Written comments by Michigan's interviewers indicate that of the 29 subjects (6.6%) who failed to produce usable magnitude response data, 5 were unable to complete the scaling tasks carried out at the end of the interview because of time constraints. Another 12 to 15 were said to be physically incapable of making line or numeric estimates because of "old age," "blindness," "arthritis," or some undisclosed disability. Our best guess is that 9 to 12 subjects (about 3% of the sample) were unable for psychological reasons to use NE or LP to make proportional judgments.

Analysis of the Matches to Social Scale Items

Employing the indirect cross-modality matching paradigm, the NE and LP matches to the social scale items are handled in exactly the same way as are the responses made to the calibration stimuli. To determine the extent to which subjects are using the two response modalities to make ratio judgments of the social stimuli, the geometric mean computed for each social scale item from the LP matches is plotted on ratio-ruled coordinates against the geometric mean for each stimulus computed from the NE matches. The cross-modal validation test predicts a unit exponent, since both LP and NE exhibit a characteristic exponent of 1.0 when matched to physical stimuli. Visual inspection of Figure 13 shows a reasonably good linear fit in log-log coordinates between measures—a power function relationship—which, of course, is what the psychophysical theory predicts because of the functional relationship presumed to hold for these modalities. The Pearson product-moment correlation between the geometric means of the line and number matches to the social items is .992, implying a high degree of linear dependence between

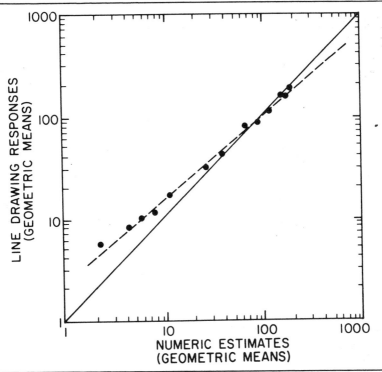

Figure 13: Line-drawing responses are plotted as a function of numeric estimates to 13 adjectival scale items implying degrees of approval-disapproval for the U.S. Supreme Court's decision on abortion. Each point represents the averaged response of 375 respondents of the Murphy-Tanenhaus national survey. The solid line is the predicted exponent of 1.0, the dashed line the empirically obtained exponent of .786.

measures.[12] This power function relationship confirms that the subjects are indeed using the two response measures to make ratio judgments of the adjectival modifiers in terms of support. The empirical exponent derived by the error-in-both-variables regression of NE to LP is .786, with 95% confidence limits for the theoretical slope from .89 to 1.12, which excludes this empirically obtained exponent.

Once again, as with the cross-modal matches to the calibrating stimuli, the relationship is obviously regressive. Recall that when the same two response modalities were brought into a functional relationship when matched to the calibrating stimuli, the exponent was similarly regressive, $NE = LP^{.879}$. The empirical exponents obtained from the matches to the social and metric stimuli are not significantly different. The social scale is attenuated because LP is regressive.

Guidelines for the Correction of Regression Bias

Cross (1974, 1981, and Lodge et al., 1975) suggests a stringent set of guidelines for deciding if and when to adjust the empirical exponent before calculating social scale values. Synoptically:

(1) The two response modalities should be highly correlated at, say .95+.

(2) The two response modalities must be linearly related on log-log coordinates, that is, be well-described by a power function.

(3) The direction of bias operating on the two response modalities must be the same in both the calibrating and social scaling tasks.

(4) The empirical exponent obtained from the matches made to the social stimuli should approximate the exponent obtained from the matches made in the calibration task to the metric stimuli.

When, as here, these standards are met, the application of Cross's regression model is warranted and the possibility of seriously distorting the social scale highly unlikely.

Calculation of Social Scale Values

Under ideal conditions, when $NE = LP^{1.0}$, the formula for computing magnitude scale values (ψ) would be:

$$\psi = (NE^{1.0}\ LP^{1.0})^{1/2}.$$

One simply raises the arithmetic mean of the logs obtained from each response modality for each stimulus to its respective power of 1.0, multiplies, and here, given two response measures for each stimulus, raises the product to .5.

To correct for bias in one or both measures, one raises the mean log value obtained from the respective matches to the social stimuli by the inverse of the exponent obtained from the matches made to the calibrating stimuli. The correction formula is simple and easy to apply:

$$\psi = (NE_1^{1/n}\ LP_2^{1/n})^{.5}$$

where n_1 is the exponent uncovered from the NE matches made to the line length stimuli in the calibrating exercise (in this study, from Figure 2, $n_1 = .988$), and n_2 is the exponent relating LP to the number stimuli (here, from Figure 11, $n_2 = .802$). Thus:

$$\psi = (NE^{1/.988}\ LP^{1/.802})^{.5}.$$

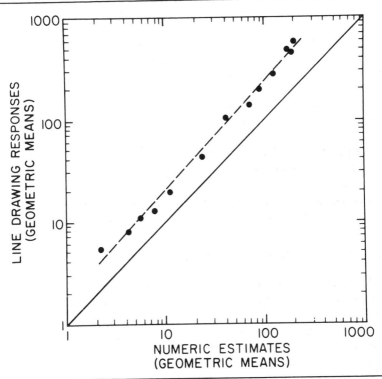

Figure 14: Line-drawing responses are plotted as a function of numeric estimates to 13 adjectival scale items implying degrees of approval-disapproval for the U.S. Supreme Court's decision on abortion. Each point represents the averaged response of 375 respondents of the Murphy-Tanenhaus national survey. The solid line is the predicted exponent of 1.0, the dashed line the empirical exponent, corrected for regression bias, of 1.11.

When the inverse of each exponent is entered into the correction factor, the effect is to raise the power exponents used to compute social scale values. Here:

$$\psi = (NE^{1.02} \, LP^{1.25})^{.5}.$$

What is important to recognize is that the empirical, corrected, and theoretical exponents are linearly related in log-log coordinates, that is, they were before, and are now after the correction, power functions of one another, and the correlation between response modalities remains exactly the same. What does change is the slope; it is tilted upward. The scale items maintain their *relative* ratio relationships to one another; only their absolute value is changed. Hence, the principal benefit of correcting for regression bias is to better approximate the "true" scale values and thereby make comparisons across studies more readily comparable.

In Figure 14 the geometric means of the LP matches to the adjectival modifiers of support are plotted as a function of the corresponding NE matches. The geomeans, pooled over the 375 survey respondents and corrected for regression bias, show a reasonably good linear fit in ratio-ruled coordinates. The correlation of .991 between measures is exactly the same as before the correction for regression. The adjusted error-in-both-variables regression of LP to NE is 1.11, with 95% confidence limits around the theoretical slope of .89 to 1.13, which includes the empirical exponent. The magnitude range of scale values, read off the corrected regression line in Figure 14, is 107:1, from "Absolutely Perfect" (ψ = 540) to "Disgusting" (ψ = 4.9). If the scale values were uncorrected for bias (as shown in Figure 13), the range of the support scale would be 37:1.

The Analysis of Individual-Level Response Data

All the analyses discussed to this point are based on group data—geometric means pooled over 10 or more subjects. Averaging is one of the most effective ways to subdue random error, but one must be cautious about pooling data, for it sometimes smothers important individual differences or hides erratic behavior.

The most direct way to look at these magnitude response data at the individual level is to compute correlation and regression coefficients for each individual and compare the results to the group averages. Figure 15 tallies the frequency of individual regression coefficients derived from each subject's NE matches to the nine line lengths and each subject's LP estimates of the nine number stimuli made in the calibration exercise. The distribution of individual exponents is regular, remarkably so given that each individual's regression exponent is obtained from a single NE and LP ratio judgment of each metric stimulus. The steep peakedness is characteristic of magnitude response data. The correlation computed for individuals averages .95 for both the NE and LP responses to the metric stimuli. The averaged regression coefficient for individuals is .99 for NE and .80 for LP, both of which closely approximate the sample average derived by the geometric mean pooled over all 375 subjects of .988 and .802. The individual response data are a good representation of the group data.

More impressive still is the distribution of individual exponents obtained from each subject's regression of LP against NE to the 13 adjectival modifiers of support. As displayed in Figure 16, the average individual correlation between magnitude response measures is .84, and the average

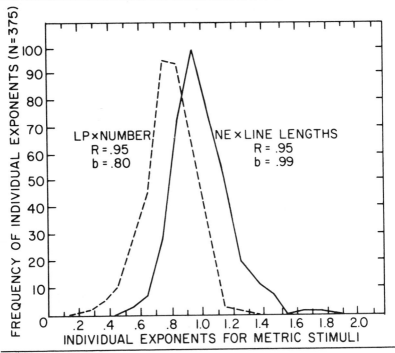

Figure 15: Frequency of individual regression exponents derived from the line-drawing and numeric estimation responses to metric stimuli obtained from each of the 375 respondents of the Murphy-Tanenhaus national survey.

regression coefficient is .87, which is not significantly different from the uncorrected slope of .79 obtained from the geometric means pooled over all 375 subjects. While some individuals obviously do better than others—as is clear for both metric and social judgments and as expected in any measurement task—the variance around the geomean is very narrow, even narrower than a normal distribution would provide.

Employing Stimulus-Type Magnitude Scales in Survey Instruments

Immediately following the magnitude scaling task, the Michigan interview proceeded conventionally. Whenever a judgment of support was called for, subjects were shown a card listing each of the 13 previously evaluated adjectival modifiers in irregular order and asked to choose that word or phrase which "best expressed their opinion" of the Supreme Court and its decisions. This routine is very similar to that used in the administration of conventionally labelled category scales. The difference, of

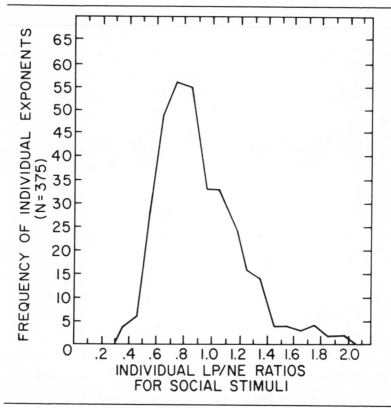

Figure 16: Frequency of individual ratios relating the line drawing to numeric estimation exponents obtained from the matches made by each of the 375 respondents in the Murphy-Tanenhaus survey to 13 adjectival descriptors of approval-disapproval for the U.S. Supreme Court's decision on abortion.

course, is that cross-modally validated magnitude weights can be assigned each response, whereas with category scaling the subject's choice among alternatives is assigned an arbitrary integer.

Problems and Prospects of the Scale-Building Approach

Analysis of the Tanenhaus-Murphy survey confirms earlier laboratory results which show that the adjectival modifiers convey metric information of support when used to evaluate political institutions, leaders, and policies. What is more, this study demonstrates that the cross-modality matching paradigm is feasible for survey research. At this juncture, then, the cross-modality matching paradigm can be used to build and validate social magnitude scales made up of instances or attributes of a social-psychological dimension, what Torgerson (1968) calls "stimulus-centered" scales. A major convenience of this scale-building approach is that once subjects have judged the amount of support implied by each scale item, the items may be presented repeatedly during the course of an interview for evaluating support for different political institutions and policies.

There are limitations to this scale-building approach as well. One problem is that in making their judgments of support subjects chose that scale item which best *approximates* their strength of opinion. Whereas the magnitude scaling of scale items is direct, that is, subjects make numeric and line-drawing responses to match the amount of support implied by each adjectival modifier, the actual expression of opinion is indirect: Subjects indicate their strength of opinion via the scale items rather than the response modalities. As a consequence, the evaluations of some subjects will predictably fall between scale items. While the magnitude weights assigned the scale items would be obviously superior to the arbitrary assignment of numbers to items measured categorically, some information is nonetheless lost.

A second, more serious problem is that all stimulus-type scales regardless of method are particularistic. The adjectival-modifier scale, for example, is specific to "support" or, perhaps, to more general expressions of "approval"-"disapproval," while most social survey instruments are omnibus instruments which routinely call for the evaluation of many different dimensions. Although this scale has not been tested sufficiently to determine its generalizability to dimensions other than support, it is obvious that the scale items are not suitable for the elicitation of quantitatively meaningful judgments across the full range of attitudinal variables found in most social science surveys.

5. THE DIRECT MAGNITUDE SCALING OF POLITICAL JUDGMENTS

An alternative to stimulus-centered scales is what we call "direct magnitude scaling." Here, rather than employ the response modalities to judge scale items on a single dimension such as support (and then have subjects choose a scale item to indicate their strength of opinion toward some institution, policy, or leader), subjects use the two response modalities within the cross-modality matching paradigm to express the magnitude of their opinion *directly* on a dimension. Essentially, whatever the scalar dimension, the stronger one's impression or preference, the greater the ratio of response to reference: the longer the line and larger the number response proportional to the reference.

The primary advantage of the direct over stimulus-scaling approach is its flexibility: Subjects can make magnitude judgments of different social phenomena on different social-psychological dimensions without first scaling dimension-specific scale items. The primary disadvantage of direct magnitude scaling is its reliance on individual rather averaged data.

To illustrate this direct approach to the magnitude scaling of social opinion and provide researchers with a basis for choosing between or mixing approaches in their research, let us spell out the procedures employed by Lodge and Tursky (1979) in their study comparing direct magnitude scaling to category scaling of the most popular variables used in the University of Michigan's 1976 National Election Study. The National Election Surveys are omnibus instruments which include a wide range of questions and incorporate examples of the most popular types and formats of category rating scales found in sociology, psychology, and political science.

General Scaling Procedures

Virtually all questions in the National Election Survey, as well as items available in compendiums for sociology, political science, and social psychology, provide bipolar options in the text of the question to establish the scalar dimension and meaningfulness of the response categories. Among the most common key words are: Approve-Disapprove, Good-Bad, Like-Dislike, More-Less, and various phrasings denoting such bipolar opposites as Liberal-Conservative and Republican-Democrat. A second characteristic of the questions in the National Election Survey and probably of all social-psychological items implying a continuum is a middle or neutral position. This "neutral" point is oftentimes stated explicitly in the text of the question by such words as "middle," "in be-tween," "so-so," "sometimes," and "more or less," or implied by a middle position on an odd-numbered category scale.

For the vast majority of existing items in the social sciences, instruction in direct magnitude scaling is straightforward. Given a subject's prior instruction and practice in making LP and NE estimates relative to a middle-ranged reference stimulus in the calibration task, specific question-by-question instructions are only required for the first three of four items in an interview before subjects are able to generalize the notion of a middle position between the polar options and make ratio responses compared to the reference position.

Survey Instructions for Direct Magnitude Scaling

Employing LP and NE in the cross-modality matching paradigm, direct magnitude scaling again involves subjects in two scaling tasks: First, the calibration of response modalities[13] and then the actual magnitude scaling of judgments.

Following the matching of NE to line lengths and LP to number stimuli in the calibration task, and a practice exercise in which subjects made LP and NE estimates of the seriousness of seven crime stimuli, the direct magnitude scaling approach proceeded in three discrete steps for each question, whatever the dimension being evaluated.

Step 1—Presentation of the Item. In this scale-confrontation study pitting category against magnitude scaling, the question was presented exactly as specified in the Codebooks for the National Election Surveys and subjects asked to choose that categorical option which they "prefer," is "closer to," "agrees with," or "best expresses your opinion," whatever the phrasing used in the question to elicit a categorical response. The purpose of this category scaling task is to have subjects indicate the *direction* of their opinion.

Step 2—Establishing a Reference Position. Each subject is now instructed to draw a reference line to represent an *"opinion in between"* the bipolar options provided by the question—a line representing a neutral position between, say, "Agree"-"Disagree," "Like"-"Dislike," "Liberal"-"Conservative," "Pro" vs "Anti" Abortion, whatever the options specified by the question. In this study we simply presented the item and below it the heading "Draw a Reference Line between X and Y," where X and Y are the polar opinions provided by the question.

Step 3—Making Ratio Responses. Relative to their reference line representing a middle position on the scalar dimension, subjects now drew a response line to express the strength of their position relative to the reference line: "How Strongly Do You Favor (Approve, etc.) X (Y)?" The stronger one's preference for "X" or "Y," the longer, proportionately, their response line to reference line. Subjects holding a middle position on the issue would draw a response line equal to their reference line.

And then on a separate page of the interview, either immediately following the line-drawing response to each question or, better yet, after making LP ratio responses to a series of related items, subjects are called on to make numeric judgments on the same questions: They first assign a reference number to represent a middle position between the X and Y options which define that continuum and then make an NE response proportional to their reference to express the magnitude of their opinion.

Here is a sampling of items drawn from the National Election Survey to illustrate how different types of questions lend themselves to the direct magnitude scaling approach. Some questions imply a comparative reference which the researcher must make explicit. For instance:

Do you basically approve or disapprove of the way Carter is handling his job as President?

_____ Approve

_____ Disapprove

In this case, we would simply ask the subject to

Draw a reference line that represents an opinion in between approve and disapprove.

REFERENCE LINE:

And then,

Now draw a response line to express the strength of your opinion. If your opinion about how Carter is handling his job as President is near the middle, in between approval and disapproval, draw a response line about the same length as your reference line. If you basically approve or disapprove, draw a response line longer than your reference line and show how much you approve or disapprove. The stronger your opinion, the longer your response line should be compared to your reference line.

RESPONSE LINE:

These extended instructions are only necessary for the first few items to establish the notion of a reference position and the notion of making comparative judgments. The average respondent soon learns, as did Gulliver in the land of Brobdingnag, that all things great and small are only so by comparison.

Most questions in social surveys explicitly state a middle position on the social psychological continuum which the researcher may use as a reference for ratio scaling. Here are some examples taken from the National Election Survey, with asterisks added to highlight the reference position:

Do you think that over the last five years your (your family's) income has gone up more than the cost of living, has fallen behind, or has stayed about even with the cost of living?

_____ Gone up more

_____ *Stayed about even

_____ Fallen behind

Some people don't pay much attention to the political campaigns. How about you, would you say that you have been very much interested in following the campaigns so far this year?

_____ Very much interested

_____ *Somewhat interested

_____ Not much interested

And this example, one of the five items used in a trust-alienation index, always elicits a robust response:

Do you think people in the government in Washington waste a lot of the money we pay in taxes, waste some of it, or don't waste very much of it?

_____ Waste a lot

_____ *Waste some

_____ Don't waste very much

Many survey questions, like those used in the National Election Survey to tap liberal-conservatism, Republican-Democratic partisan identification, and people's preferences for different public policies, ask respondents to place themselves on a 7-point category scale. To insure the independence between measures and avoid confusing shifts between magnitude and categorical judgments, it is recommended that subjects first make LP judgments to a set of related items, then make their NE estimates of the same items, and last make categorical judgments. Let this final example, one of several policy-preference items typical of those employed in the election surveys, illustrate the sequence of scaling tasks employed in the Lodge-Tursky scale-confrontation study:

Some people believe that we should spend much less money for defense. Others feel that defense spending should be increased. And, of course, some other people have opinions somewhere in between.

Compared to the government's present level of defense spending, do you think we should increase defense spending, keep it about the same as now, or decrease defense spending?

_____ Increase defense spending

_____ *Same as now

_____ Decrease defense spending

64

Draw a Reference Line to represent the federal government's present level of defense spending.

REFERENCE LINE:

Now, compared to the reference line which represents what the government is spending now on defense, draw a Response Line to say how much you favor an increase (decrease) in defense spending.

RESPONSE LINE:

Given these instructions, subjects would give proportionately longer lines and bigger numbers to express the strength of their position on the question of defense spending: The more strongly they favored their position—whether an increase or decrease—the larger their response-to-reference ratio. Later, following the line-drawing responses to each of the different policy questions, this procedure was repeated for subjects to make numeric estimates of opinion strength and repeated again for subjects to make categorical responses on a 7-point category scale.

Calculation of Scale Values

The construction of magnitude scale values from the direct responses to each question is a simple procedure. Since two ratios are created by each subject to each question—one for the response line to reference line and one for the response number to reference number—two ratios for each individual are the basic units of analysis. The calculation of scale values merely involves computing the two response-to-reference ratios separately for each subject to each question. The direction of response, whether the subject favors more or less defense spending, is known from his or her initial categorical response. To reflect direction of response in the ratios, one simply takes the inverse of the LP and NE ratios for one of the bipolar options, here, for example, for a "decrease" in defense spending.

Let one example suffice here for the computation of ratios, since the procedures described earlier for the scale-building approach are logically identical. Suppose that the subject, having first indicated categorically that he or she thinks of himself or herself as a "Democrat," draws a 10 mm long reference line to represent a middle position on the continuum between Republican and Democrat and then draws a 100 mm response line to express his or her strength of partisanship—a 10:1 LP ratio of response to reference. And later when called on to make numeric estimates, he or she assigns the number 5 as a reference number and, say, the number 40 as a response, for an 8:1 NE ratio of response to reference. Once again, it is standard practice to work in logs when dealing with magnitude judgments.

Thus, when transformed into logs, this subject's response-to-reference LP ratio of 100:10 is computed as 2 - 1 = 1, which when exponentiated is 10, for a 10:1 LP ratio score of partisan strength. For a subject's NE judgments of 40:5, the log transform yields 1.6 - .7 = .9, which when exponentiated equals a 7.9:1 NE ratio score of partisan strength. An averaged magnitude scale value for this subject on this variable is obtained by taking the arithmetic mean of the two ratios: $(10 + 7.9)/2 = 8.95:1$.

The Plotting and Analysis of Direct Magnitude Judgments

For direct magnitude scaling—unlike the scale-building approach in which subjects judge a series of attributes on a scalar dimension, with each point on the plot representing the pooled estimates of all subjects to each attribute, here each subject is represented by a single LP ratio score on one axis and a single NE ratio score on the other axis. Correlation and regression coefficients are then calculated across *individuals* for each question rather than between the geometric means of pooled responses for all subjects to a series of scale items.

To illustrate the application of direct magnitude scaling to the measurement of social judgments, and show how the results can be used to test hypotheses, let us focus on the partisan identification question since it is a central variable in electoral research. Figure 17 plots on log-log coordinates the ratio measures of Republican-Democratic partisanship obtained from each of 211 subjects in the Lodge-Tursky survey. Each point on the plot represents the conjoint LP and NE response-to-reference ratio of *each* individual.

Given that we are working with single subjects expressing their individual strength of partisanship, we may well have expected a scatter of points resembling the random pattern of pigeon droppings in St. Mark's Square. Rather, as is clear by visual inspection of the scatterplot, the relationship between the LP and NE ratio expressions of partisanship across the 211 subjects is fairly described as linear in ratio-ruled coordinates, thereby confirming a consensually conceived quantitative dimension underlying partisanship. The correlation between the LP and NE ratios is .90, with an error-in-both-variables regression coefficient of .94.

The results for the party identification question are typical of each of the 28 political variables included in this survey (Lodge and Tursky, 1979). On average, correlation coefficients hover around .92, regression coefficients range between .90 and 1.02, and the fit between ratio response measures is reasonably described as linear in logarithmically ruled coordinates. Although the correlation coefficients are weaker and the fit of theoretical equation to empirical data less good than we have come to expect from the stimulus-scaling approach, it must be kept in mind that

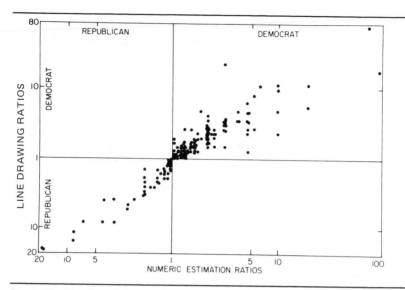

Figure 17: Line-drawing estimates plotted as a function of numeric estimates of strength of partisanship on ratio-ruled coordinates. Each point on the plot is the conjoint LP and NE response-to-reference ratio for each of the 211 individual respondents in the Lodge-Tursky (1979) survey (reprinted by permission).

this direct scaling procedure relies on the single scores of individuals rather than their pooled estimates for a set of scale items. The overall effect is a 4% to 5% decrease in explained variance when compared to the scale-building approach which, in turn, is 7% to 10% less than routinely found in sensory psychophysical experiments.

Before turning to an illustration of how these ratio response data can be used in testing hypotheses, a brief aside relating magnitude to categorical judgments will help set the stage for contrasting the two methods in terms of their relative power in social science research. There is, as displayed in Figure 17, about a 90:1 range of partisanship experessed when subjects are provided magnitude response measures. The (geometric) mean-to-mean magnitude range from Republican to Democrat identification averages out to 15:1. What happens when these same judgments are measured by the standard 7-point category scale? Figure 18 compares in semilog coordinates the category against ratio measures of partisanship obtained from all 211 subjects. The point for each magnitude response is the arithmetic mean of their LP and NE ratios combined, and the lines surrounding each point represent ± one standard deviation of the mean.

As is apparent from this display, there is a broad range of partisanship within each category level, with the greatest amount of variance occurring in the endmost categories, thereby indicating that the most partisan respondents are the most constrained by the arbitrary restrictions imposed

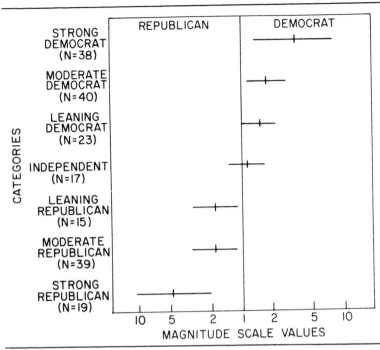

Figure 18: Comparison of categorical to ratio estimates of strength of partisanship plotted on semilog coordinates for respondents in the Lodge-Tursky (1979) survey. The point on each line is the geometric mean of the LP and NE ratios of all respondents making that specific categorical response. The line surrounding each point is ± one standard deviation of the mean (reprinted by permission).

by this standard category scale. Further, it is clear that the categories are not intervally spaced: "Leaning" and "Moderate" partisans are closer to one another than are "Moderate" and "Strong" partisans. In fact, it is impossible to distinguish those who chose either the "Leaning" or "Not so strong" labels.

Because the expression of partisan strength is arbitrarily constrained by the standard 7-point category scale, we see in Figure 18 how category scaling costs information and misclassifies respondents. Essentially, Figure 18 illustrates that when the range of categories available to respondents for expressing their opinion is small relative to the magnitude of their opinion strength, most of the distortion occurs in the end categories. This is particularly serious because many theories of behavior posit a relationship between strength of opinion and the likelihood of a congruent behavior: Those expressing the strongest beliefs and preferences are most likely to behave in accord with their opinion, while those who are less strongly engaged are least likely to act on behalf of their opinions. Because of the wide range of opinion which we observe in the endmost categories, a researcher cannot be confident that a respondent choosing a polar category is expressing a moderate or intense opinion. Attempts, therefore, to predict subsequent behavior as a function of categorical expressions of opinion strength will, predictably, experience poor results solely as a consequence of the arbitrary constraints imposed by category scales.

Analysis of Ratio Relationships

To illustrate how these ratio judgments could be used in social science applications, let us offer a simple example taken from the Lodge-Tursky study. This survey was carried out in two waves: once in May 1976 immediately before the New York State presidential primaries, with 108 subjects, and again in October 1976 just prior to the election, with 103 subjects. Both surveys asked subjects for their party identification and candidate preferences. In these analyses we will focus on the two main contenders—(then-) President Gerald Ford and the major challenger, Jimmy Carter.

Figure 19 plots strength of candidate preference as a function of partisan strength in ratio-ruled coordinates for the May sample. The value of 1 on each axis is the neutral (reference) position. Each point on the graph relates the mean of each subject's LP and NE ratio for party identification to the mean of his LP and NE ratio of candidate preference. The correlation between variables is quite strong, .83, but more important it is possible to examine the slope of the relationship. The best-fitting function relating candidate preference to party identification for the May sample is a power function with a slope of 1.4: A twofold increase in party identification produces a 2.8-fold increase in candidate support.

In October, just prior to the election (Figure 20), the correlation is again high, .81, virtually the same as for May, but with a significant steepening of the power function exponent to 2.0. Here, in the week immediately preceding the election, party identification exerts a stronger impact on candidate preference: A twofold increase in party identification produces a fourfold increase in preference for a candidate.

Although the data from this survey are not ideal, the change in relationship between candidate preference and party identification illustrates the general argument. The relationship between variables changed between May and October, presumably as a function of the presidential campaign. The presidential campaign did not appreciably affect the correlation between variables (.83 in May, .81 in October), but did strengthen the preference for one's party candidate (a change in slope from 1.4 to 2.0). The change in slope is primarily a function of an increase in the standard deviation for magnitude judgments of candidate preference, from .688 to

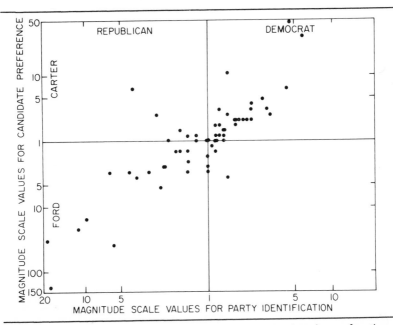

Figure 19: Candidate preference for Ford versus Carter is plotted as a function of strength of partisanship on ratio-ruled coordinates. Each point on the graph represents the conjoint LP and NE reference-to-response ratio on each variable for each of the 108 respondents in the May 1976 Lodge-Tursky (1979) survey (reprinted by permission).

.838, while the variance for Party Identification decreased only slightly from .494 to .422.

When an investigator is interested in the magnitude of change in a relationship between variables—how much an exponent increases or decreases as a function of some experimental manipulation or real world intervention (campaign effects implied here)—magnitude scaling methods prove to be superior to category scaling because category scaling does not provide quantitative measures of opinion strength.

6. COMPARING CATEGORY TO MAGNITUDE SCALES OF SOCIAL OPINION

Conventional category scaling rarely if ever provides quantitative measurement of opinion strength. The empirical results reported throughout this volume for both social and sensory stimuli indicate that category scaling does not produce regression coefficients which can be meaning-

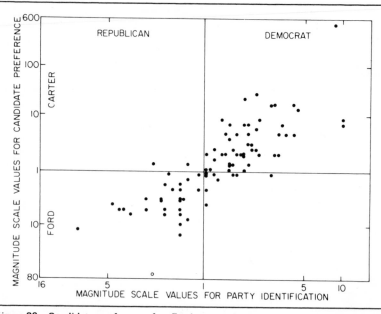

Figure 20: Candidate preference for Ford versus Carter is plotted as a function of strength of partisanship on ratio-ruled coordinates. Each point on the graph represents the conjoint LP and NE reference-to-response ratio on each variable for each of the 103 respondents in the October 1976 Lodge-Tursky (1979) survey (reprinted by permission).

fully interpreted as quantitative expressions of the relationship between variables. Regression coefficients are arbitrary when produced by variables measured categorically because of the arbitrariness of the categorical measure—first, in the number of categories imposed by the format of the scale and, second, in the numbers assigned to the categories. The number of categories imposed by the format of the category scale and the numbers assigned the categories arbitrarily fix the value of the regression coefficient. If one were to compute a regression coefficient for two variables which were in perfect linear agreement across the full range of values, the obtained slope would be a function of the number of categories, not the true magnitude of relationship between variables. Under ideal conditions two linearly related 7-point scales will produce a slope of about 1.0, while the same two variables—again in linear agreement, one measured on a 10-point scale, the other on a 5-point scale—will yield a slope about .5. Relatedly, the numbers assigned the categories will alter the slope.

The central problem is of course that category scaling is oblivious to the true range of stimuli and the subjective range of opinion. Because the range of response is fixed, category scales cannot adjust to changes in the true range of stimuli or track the magnitude of opinion strength.

Because the range of social stimuli is not known beforehand, varies from question to question, and varies across individuals, category scaling denies effective access to a quantitative measure of change in the relationship between variables. Regression coefficients computed from categorical judgments are indeterminate; essentially, where the stimulus range is greater than the response range, the slope will be lower than it should be, and where the stimulus range is less than the response range, the slope will be steeper than it should be—solely as a result of the arbitrary constraints imposed by the format of the scale. Because all the category scales compared in these scale-confrontation studies provide a far smaller range than the opinion ranges they purport to measure, and because magnitude measures track the stimulus range relatively well as a result of the lack of constraints upon the respondent, one routinely finds (see Note 6) that the regression coefficient for category scales numbered in the conventional fashion is lower than that obtained with magnitude measures (Curtis, 1970; Ward, 1972; Marks, 1974).

Given the power of regression analysis in social science research, Tufte (1969) and others (Heise, 1975; Namboodiri et al., 1975) suggest that investigators assign numbers to the categories which use their knowledge about the meaning of the responses to reflect more accurately the true relationships between the responses. The first problem with this recommendation is the arbitrariness of the method; it depends upon some consensus among researchers as to the meaning of responses and agreement on the numbers assigned to the categories. The second problem is that the movement in the social sciences toward 7-point category scales with only the endpoints labelled makes it difficult to do other than assume that the categories are equally spaced.

Now comes the debate: What are the consequences of treating categorical data as if they were interval? Some researchers (e.g., Wilson, 1971; Marks, 1974) argue that the use of interval-level statistics with ordinal-level data is neither legitimate nor empirically tenable, citing as evidence numerous experimental studies which show that violations of the interval assumptions make it impossible to test or choose between competitive models. Other researchers (e.g., Bohrnstedt and Carter, 1971; Labovitz, 1970) argue that regression analysis is so robust that the violation of interval assumptions does not usually lead to serious errors in parameter estimation or curve fitting. A middle position, argued by Asher (1976), is that the violation of interval-level assumptions is consequential only when violations are "extreme"—when, for example, the subjective range of the stimuli is broad or the range of the category rating scale constricted.

What constitutes a too-broad range of stimuli or too-narrow range of response categories cannot be specified in advance, and the failure to model the interaction between stimulus and range effects is a primary cause for the contradictory recommendations (Marks, 1968). When we go back and examine closely the 100 or so plots between category and magnitude scales of social stimuli obtained from the studies reviewed in this volume (see Figure 5 as an example), it is sometimes the case that although the overall relationship between scale types is markedly curvilinear, one can sometimes detect a linear relationship between variables in the middle of the scale, say within the middle 5:1 or even 10:1 range of the scale. This linear segment within a curvilinear relationship is commonly observed in sensory psychophysical scales of physical stimuli as well (Stevens and Galanter, 1957), indicating that within "moderate" 5:1 to 10:1 stimulus ranges the violation of interval assumptions will not be serious. However, all the magnitude data for social variables reviewed in this volume exceed this moderate range: On average, the magnitude range of opinion strength for political parties, candidates, and issues is about 60:1. As a rule of thumb: The greater the discrepancy between the magnitude range of the stimuli and the imposed range of the measurement scale, the greater the deviation of categorical data from interval-level assumptions, and therefore the more consequential the effects of treating ordinal data as if they were interval.

Unfortunately, there is no feasible method available today for deriving interval data from category rating scales because (in addition to the problems inherent in the very act of categorization) the subjective range of social stimuli varies from individual to individual from issue to issue over time, while the response range of the category scale is arbitrarily fixed. Almost invariably, magnitude scales prove superior to category scales because category scaling artifactually constrains people's judgments, while the magnitude measures are relatively free of this constraint. When, as is typical, the subjective range of people's impressions exceeds the category response range, the relationship between the category and magnitude scale will be curvilinear, concave downward. If, on the other hand, the subjective range of the stimuli is less than the category response range (as would be the case if the National Election Survey employed a 100-point category scale), the relationship between scales would again be curvilinear, but convex. Based on these characteristic results, we see that the major substantive effect of using category scales to measure social beliefs and preferences is to truncate strong opinions.

7. RESEARCH DECISIONS

Given the power of magnitude scaling, one may well ask why category scaling retains its dominant position in social science research. Two arguments in support of category scaling are voiced most frequently in social science circles: The first is the issue of comparability, the second is the question of survey costs, in particular interview time. To assess the relative costs and benefits of the two scaling methods, let us address both these arguments, then evaluate various time-saving alternatives to the cross-modality matching paradigm, and conclude with a discussion of the key issue—the relative utility of magnitude and category scaling.

Comparability

Category scaling enjoys widespread contemporary use, with some items and formats used in the social sciences dating back to the 1930s. Acknowledging the desirability of repeated measures for longitudinal studies, the use of magnitude scaling in social research need not necessarily effect a break with the past. Because magnitude scales are ratio-level scales, one could convert measures of magnitude into intervally spaced categories. A more reasonable strategy—as described in the section on direct scaling—would be to include both category and magnitude scales in the same interview instrument, since some form of categorization is a requisite first step in direct magnitude scaling. A researcher could—as was done in our local-area survey—employ conventional category scales to establish the scalar dimension and direction of a subject's response and thereby maintain comparability with past items as well as gain the capacity to compare and contrast measures.

Time Costs

Within the cross-modality matching paradigm, magnitude scaling requires more interview time than does conventional category scaling. The Tanenhaus-Murphy survey administered by the University of Michigan's Survey Research Center took on average 18 minutes per respondent for the calibration of the NE and LP response modalities and cross-modal scaling of the 13 support scale items. Once these tasks were completed, the interview schedule proceeded conventionally: In response to a question, the subject chose that word or phrase which best expressed his or her opinion about the Court, its decisions, and performance. This evaluation task takes about the same amount of time as does conventional category scaling.

Based on our survey experience, the direct scaling approach costs in time: 6 to 7 minutes per subject for the calibration of number and line responses, 5 to 6 minutes of instruction and practice in the use of LP and NE to make proportional judgments of social variables, and 12 to 25 seconds for subjects to make line and number responses per question. Were the choice of scaling method decided solely in terms of time, category scaling is more cost effective.

Alternative Strategies to the
Cross-Modality Matching Paradigm

Given the high costs of survey research, many researchers opt for one or another time-saving variant of magnitude scaling, relegating the cross-modality matching paradigm to laboratory and methodological studies. Far and away the most popular magnitude scaling approach is to drop the calibration procedure and employ one response measure, typically numeric estimation. Let us describe and evaluate these and related alternatives to the cross-modality matching paradigm, for some magnitude scaling approaches are decidedly stronger than others.

Skipping the Calibration Procedure. The calibration procedure is first and foremost a practice exercise and vehicle for instruction in magnitude scaling. Without some instruction and practice in using the response measure(s) to make proportional judgments, some subjects would make ordinal judgments. The key question, then, is not "to calibrate or not to calibrate" but how much of what kind of practice? The advantage of calibrating the response(s) against metric stimuli is that a researcher can then determine whether the subjects are using the responses properly to make proportional judgments and if so how accurately, and given the four guidelines proposed in Chapter 4, correct for regression bias. This information becomes critical should the social scale fail the criterion-test established for the psychophysical validation of magnitude scales.

Given the cognitive ambiguity of social stimuli and their lack of objectively measured properties, there are, invariably, alternative explanations for why a given scale may have failed: First to mind, perhaps the subjects failed to use the response modalities properly to make magnitude judgments, or, perhaps, the scalar dimension is multidimensional, or, perhaps, the stimuli are not perceived as attributes on a quantitative dimension. If, on the basis of the calibration data, it can be shown that subjects are indeed making proportional judgments of the calibrating metric, critical attention rightfully shifts from the competence of the respondents to make ratio judgments to the characteristics of the social scale itself. The calibration procedure is therefore important, if not necessary, in social scaling applications, whether a researcher employs one or two response modalities in the social scaling task.

One Response Measure Without Calibration. A second time-saving alternative to the cross-modality matching paradigm employs one rather than two magnitude response measures. Upward of 95% of all sensory and social psychophysical studies employ one measure, typically numeric estimation. Employing NE alone (without a formal calibration task) would require 4 to 5 minutes of instruction and practice per respondent and 5 to 12 seconds per numeric response, more than halving the time required for the full cross-modality matching paradigm. What one gives up—in addition to the ability to average the two responses and thereby reduce the random error involved in measurement[14]—is the capacity to psychophysically validate the social magnitude scale.

Despite the popularity of this magnitude scaling approach, the sole reliance on one uncalibrated response measure is the weakest of several alternative strategies for social science research. Where theory is strong, the social stimuli and scalar dimensions well-defined, and the empirical relationships between variables well-established, researchers could credibly compare their results to a set of consensual norms. Where, however, these conditions are not met, the results obtained from this simple magnitude scaling approach must be accepted or rejected on the basis of face and construct validity checks.

The Use of One Calibrated Response Measure. A stronger introduction of magnitude scaling into social science research could be accomplished by employing one response measure which is calibrated against a metric. Employing numeric estimation, for example, a researcher would first have subjects match numbers to, say, line lengths, then have subjects match numbers to the social scale items or have them use numbers directly to express the strength of their opinions.

This simple inclusion of a formal calibration task in the study design would increase survey time by 6 to 7 minutes, but decidedly enhance the power of the study. If the single response modality were calibrated, a researcher could then demonstrate that the subjects understood the concept of proportionality and used the response modality to make proportional judgments. What is *assumed*, of course, is that subjects applied their acquired skills in making ratio judgments of metric stimuli on a sensory continuum to the ratio scaling of social stimuli on a social-psychological dimension. Researchers are of course more ready to make and accept such assumptions than are their critics.

This calibrated single-measure approach would be strengthened further by incorporating the cross-modality matching paradigm into the study design. A researcher could, for example, use number estimation and line production to psychophysically validate the scale on a representative subsample and then employ numeric estimation as a single magnitude response measure for the bulk of the sample. This strategy appreciably reduces the costs of the complete cross-modality matching paradigm and offers distinct advantages over other single-modality approaches. First and foremost, it allows the researcher to *indirectly* confirm or disconfirm the interval validity of the scale by comparing the scale values obtained from the full sample to those obtained from the subsample. This design appears to be the most powerful alternative to the full-fledged cross-modality matching paradigm.[15]

8. CONCLUSION:
THE RELATIVE UTILITY OF
MAGNITUDE OVER CATEGORY SCALES

No one, of course, favors weak, crude measurement, so the issue between category and magnitude scaling ultimately turns on the question of utility—the relative worth of the two scaling methods in the description, prediction, and explanation of social phenomena. The reliance on category scaling appears to compromise the full range of social science research activity from the simple description of opinion distributions to the formal modeling of preferences and behavior.

Perhaps the most serious consequence of crude measurement is weak theory. Given ordinal-level measurement, one is unable to test quantitative hypotheses: One can state only that Y "depends on" X to some extent. The magnitude of effect of X on Y cannot be specified. What is lost is a sensitive, quantitatively meaningful measure of the relationship between variables. What is lost is the capacity to determine the form of functional relationships or measure the impact of change on relationships.

The ultimate test of magnitude scaling, or any measure, method, or model, is its practical utility—its predictive and explanatory power. To date, most of the effort in social magnitude scaling (ours included) has been spent demonstrating problems with category scaling and extolling the virtues of linear functions on ratio-ruled coordinates. This was perhaps to be expected given the obvious problems with category scaling and the radical departure from conventional practice in the social sciences represented by magnitude scaling. There are, at last, efforts now being made to directly address the question of utility.

One of the most promising approaches involves the use of multiple magnitude response measures within LISREL (for Linear Structural Relationships) models. Introduced by Jöreskog (1973, 1977) and elegantly described by Bentler (1980), LISREL offers a dramatic improvement over ordinary regression analyses in the modeling of behavior. LISREL is designed to estimate causal effects in structural equations while, at the same time, separating errors in equations (residuals) from errors in variables (measurement error). What is particularly noteworthy—and what may well turn out to be a strong impetus for the broader use of magnitude scaling in social science research—is that LISREL relies on multiple, independent measures of the variables in the structural equation model.

The initial work in this area—incorporating category and magnitude measures of social variables within LISREL—is being done in the Netherlands by Willem Saris and his associates (1980). A principal finding to date is a 12% to 15% increase in explained variance for magnitude over categorical measures, a consequence primarily of the large amounts of measurement error stemming from categorical measures. What has yet to be explored systematically—work is now in progress—is the extent to which the problems associated with categorical measures allow acceptance of models which would, had the variables been better measured, be found to be unacceptable.

These and other rigorous tests comparing categorical to magnitude measures are critically important, for it is a truism of science—I know of no exception—that established methods, no matter how weak, are never abandoned until a better method is ready in its stead.

NOTES

1. Logarithms, originally developed by mathematicians for dealing with large numbers in complex problems, were later found to be helpful in mathematical descriptions of many natural phenomena, including the behavior of psychophysical judgments. Using logs allows multiplication, division, and exponentiation (raising to a power) to be replaced by the respectively simpler operations of addition, subtraction, and multiplication. The basic rules for math with logs are:

(1) Multiplication is replaced by addition: $\log(x \cdot y) = \log(X) + \log(Y)$. For example, the log of 6 (.778) plus the log of 2 (.301) = 1.08, which is the log of 12.
(2) Division is replaced by subtraction: $\log(x \div y) = \log(X) - \log(Y)$. For example, the log of 6 (.778) minus the log of 2 (.301) = .477, which is the log of 3.
(3) Exponentiation is replaced by multiplication: $\log(X^n) = n \cdot \log X$. For example, the log of 6 (.778) times 2 = 1.556, which is the log of 36.

Another benefit of working with logs is access to logarithmically ruled graphs, which, as shown in Figure 1, automatically transform equal distance (log cycles) into equal ratios (1-10, 10-100, 100-1000).

2. While not a "true" ratio scale $(Y = aX + 0)$ in that the zero point is arbitrary, these scales preserve proportionality and, hence, are amenable to higher order statistics. See Marks (1976) for a thorough discussion of where magnitude scaling fits into a general typology of scales.

3. See Stevens and Galanter (1957) and Eisler (1962) for a systematic description of the whys and wherefores for this characteristic relationship between category and magnitude scales. And see Marks (1968, 1974), Shinn (1974), and Wegener (1981) for a mathematical treatment of why category scales fail to track the magnitude of stimulus intensity.

4. Omitted from this discussion are several important tests of the internal validity of scales, perhaps the most important being the "additivity assumption," here, the extent to which the magnitude weights for thefts add up when combined with degrees of threat and injury to the victim. The topic is technically and substantively complex. See Sellin and Wolfgang (1964) and Coleman and Rainwater (1978) for a discussion of the problem and analyses.

5. Stated more formally, if the sensation of the first response modality, R_1, is related to the stimulus S by a power function with a characteristic exponent of a

$$R_1 = S_1^a$$

and if the sensation of the second modality used in the cross-matching procedure is related to the same set of stimuli by its own characteristic exponent b

$$R_2 = S_1^b$$

when R_1 and R_2 are matched to the values of S we can substitute stimulus values so that

$$S_1{}^a = S_2{}^b$$

then, by taking the logarithm of each side of the equation, we can write

$$a \log S_1 = b \log S_2$$

or

$$\log S = (a/b) \log S_2.$$

When the values are plotted in log-log coordinates, this equation represents a straight line, a power function, with the slope of the line equal to the a/b ratio of the original exponents.

6. A technical note addressed to colleagues who argue for the logarithmic transformation of categorical data is included here. The curve drawn through each plot represents the best-fitting logarithmic function. However, and this is a typical finding, it is ambiguous whether a log or power function best represents this curvilinear relationship between category and magnitude scales. When categorical data are plotted in appropriately transformed coordinates in order to linearize the relationships for the purpose of estimating function parameters, it is clear that either function would do as well. When plotted in linear-log coordinates to test for a logarithmic function, the category values are linear with log magnitude values with coefficients of linear regression varying between .98 and .996. When next plotted in log-log coordinates to test for a power function, the regression is also linear with equally good linear corrections of .98 and exponents ranging between .44 and .48. These findings are in line with Marks's (1968) analyses which show that the empirical exponent of the power function relationship between category and magnitude scales depends on both the stimulus range and the number of category responses provided by the scale. Summarily, as the range of responses used in the category scale approaches the magnitude range of the stimuli, the two scales approach linear agreement. Unfortunately, the "true" range of social stimuli is unknown beforehand and varies across issues, over time, and between individuals, thereby making it impossible to choose the appropriate category scale format.

7. Bernd Wegener (1981) of the Zentrum für Umfragen, Methoden und Analysen of the University of Mannheim, West Germany, recently carried out a series of political surveys employing numeric estimation and line drawing in the cross-modality matching paradigm using a standard sized (8.5 × 11″) survey format. By instructing respondents to draw multiple line responses if necessary to express their strength of opinion, he found little evidence of regression bias on LP within this standard format.

8. Measuring line-drawing responses is tiresome, an intellectually vacuous task, despite what seasoned scholars say about the benefits of sticking close to the data. Commercial devices are now available for digitizing line lengths. When plugged into a microprocessor, the lines are measured to an accuracy of a tenth of a millimeter and the length of response stored in memory for analyses.

9. Computer packages for the social sciences such as SPSS do not provide a geometric mean function. The conversion of response data to logs is available as an SPSS option and the computation of the arithmetic mean of the logs can be outputted by the Condescriptive Command, Statistics All, requiring then that the researcher exponentiate the mean on a hand calculator to obtain the geometric mean.

10. Were we to calculate scale values for the metric stimuli based on this empirical exponent of .879, the objective 100:1 range of the metric stimuli would be attenuated to a

45:1 range. (Read the magnitude values off the empirical regression line: 250/5.6 = 45:1.) By the same token, if the same pattern of regression were uncovered for the LP responses to social stimuli, the attentuation effect would truncate the social scale values.

11. Psychophysicists typically "eyeball" the plot to determine whether the scatter of points is linear on log-log coordinates and whether the empirical exponent is a good first-order approximation of the theoretical exponent. One can construct 95% confidence limits around the theoretical exponent to determine the closeness of fit. The formula for calculating 95% confidence limits for the errors-in-both-variables regression model is:

$$(\beta)\left(\tan 45° \pm \arcsin\left[\left\{\frac{t}{r} \quad \frac{1-r^2}{n-2}\right\}^{\frac{1}{2}}\right]\right)$$

where

t = the value of Student's t for α = .05 and df = n − 2,

r = the product-moment correlation between the two dependent variables,

n = the number of data points in the regression plot.

12. Because measures of explained variance are insensitive to gentle departures from the equation being fitted to data, psychophysicists rarely report correlation coefficients. Hamblin calculated r^2's for a sampling of both sensory and social psychophysical studies and reports that for sensory scales "in most instances the variance explained by the theoretical function is .99+ for data pooled or averaged for ten or more observers, and .95+ for a single set of data for just one observer" (1974: 69), while the r^2's for magnitude scales of social status are typically on the order of .95 for grouped data, and about .90 for the judgments of individuals (1974: 73, 91, 93). These estimates of explained variance are representative as well of the scale-building studies carried out to date in our laboratory and in field research.

13. The calibration task employed in this survey is similar to that described earlier. A total of 211 local area adults drew lines to a sequence of nine number stimuli and made numeric estimates of an identical set of nine line length values relative to a middle-ranged reference. The only change in the calibration task was procedural: Rather than arbitrarily set the reference number 50 for numeric estimates and fix a 50 mm reference line for line drawing, subjects were instructed to give the first stimulus any line or number response they felt "appropriate" or "comfortable with" to make proportionately larger and smaller line and numeric estimates of the calibrating stimuli. This free-assignment procedure (identical to the prototypical instructions reprinted early in Chapter 2) is employed increasingly through-out psychophysics as it tends to generate less regression bias than does the assignment of an investigator-imposed reference. (The procedure can, of course, be adapted for stimulus-scaling as well by allowing subjects to give the first item, for example, "so-so," any reference number or line length they feel is appropriate.) The computation, analysis, and plotting of calibration response data are identical to that described earlier. Most social-psychological studies continue the older practice of assigning a fixed reference value, assuming that it helps subjects learn to make proportional judgments. In several comparisons of the two methods, we have found only minimal differences between the fixed and free-assignment procedure.

14. As a multivariate scaling approach, the use of two response modalities within the cross-modality matching paradigm offers several advantages over the traditional repeated measures design in which subjects use the same type of response, say a category scale, to evaluate the same stimulus twice (Cross, 1981). Although repeated measures are intended

to reduce measurement-error variance and thereby provide more reliable estimates of opinion, there are several problems with the use of repeated measures which are minimized if not eliminated by the multivariate design. (1) Successive measures with the same response measure are frequently not independent: Subjects may be able to recall their previous (categorical) response when presented with the same stimulus, and thereby appear overly consistent. The use of two separate response modalities (say LP and NE) minimizes these memory effects. (2) When presented with the same item twice, subjects may become bored and provide increasingly less reliable answers over the course of an interview. With multivariate measures, interest may be sustained longer. (3) Finally, and most important, employing two different psychophysical response modalities provides a powerful criterion validity test which goes well beyond the simple reliability measure obtained from repeated measures.

15. A superficially related, but decidedly weaker alternative to the cross-modality matching paradigm would be to psychophysically validate the scale on a representative sample and then simply assign these magnitude weights to the scale items in subsequent surveys. For the sample proper, the items could be presented in much the same way as were the adjectival modifiers in the Tanenhaus-Murphy study. The problem with this approach, in addition to the lack of any direct or indirect validity test, is that subjects, having never evaluated the items in terms of magnitude, may well treat the items as categories on an ordinal scale.

REFERENCES

ASHER, H. (1976) Causal Modeling. Sage University Papers Series on Quantitative Applications. Beverly Hills, CA: Sage.

BENTLER, P. M. (1980) "Multivariate analyses with latent variables: Causal modeling." Annual Review of Psychology 31: 419-456.

BLALOCK, H. (1960) Social Statistics. New York: McGraw-Hill.

BOHRNSTEDT, G. W. and T. M. CARTER (1971) "Robustness in regression analysis," in H. L. Costner (ed.), Sociological Methodology 1971. San Francisco: Jossey-Bass.

CLIFF, N. (1973) "Scaling." Annual Review of Psychology 24: 473-506.

COCHRANE, R. and A. ROBERTSON (1973) "The Life Events Inventory: A measure of the relative severity of psycho-social stressors." Journal of Psychosomatic Research 135-139.

COLEMAN, R. and L. RAINWATER (1978) Social Standing in America: New Dimensions of Class. New York: Basic Books.

CORSON, W. H. (1970) "Conflict and Cooperation in East-West Crises: Dynamics of Crisis Intervention." Ph.D. dissertation, Harvard University.

CROSS, D. V. (1981) "On judgments of magnitude," in B. Wegener (ed.), Social Attitudes and Psychophysical Measurement. Hillsdale, NJ: Erlbaum.

CROSS, D. V. (1974) "Some technical notes on psychophysical scaling," in H. Moskowitz et al. (eds.), Sensation and Measurement: Papers in Honor of S. S. Stevens. Dordrecht, Netherlands: Reidel.

CROSS, D. V. (1973) "Sequential dependencies and regression in psychophysical judgments." Perception & Psychophysics 14: 547-552.

CURTIS, D. W. (1970) "Magnitude estimations and category judgments of brightness and brightness intervals: A two-state interpretation." Journal of Experimental Psychology 83: 201-208.

DAWSON, W. E. and R. P. BRINKER (1971) "Validation of ratio scales of opinion by multimodality matching." Perception & Psychophysics 9: 413-417.

EISLER, H. (1962) "On the problem of category scales in psychophysics." Scandinavian Journal of Psychology 3: 81-87.

EKMAN, G. (1962) "Measurement of moral judgment: A comparison of scaling methods." Perceptual and Motor Skills 15: 3-9.

EKMAN, G. and T. KUENNAPAS (1963) "A further study of direct and indirect scaling methods." Scandinavian Journal of Psychology 4: 77-80.

FIGLIO, R. M. (1978) The National Survey of Crime Severity: Result of the Pretest. Monograph, Department of Criminology, University of Pennsylvania.

FIGLIO, R. M. (1976) "The seriousness of offenses: An evaluation by offenders and non-offenders." Journal of Criminal Law and Criminology 66: 189-200.

FINNIE, B. and R. D. LUCE (1960) Magnitude Estimation, Pair Comparison, and Successive Interval Scales of Attitude Items. Monograph, Department of Psychology, University of Pennsylvania.

HAMBLIN, R. L. (1974) "Social attitudes: Magnitude meaurement and theory," in H. M. Blalock, Jr. (ed.), Measurement in the Social Sciences. Chicago: Aldine.

HEISE, D. R. (1975) Causal Analysis. New York: John Wiley.

HOLMES, T. H. and R. H. RAHE (1967) "The Social Readjustment Rating Scale." Journal of Psychosomatic Research 11: 213-218.

JÖRESKOG, K. G. (1977) "Structural equation models in the social sciences: Specification, estimation, and testing," in P. R. Krishnaiah (ed.), Application of Statistics. The Hague, Netherlands: North Holland Publishing Co.

JÖRESKOG, K. G. (1973) "A general method for estimating a linear structural equation system," in A. S. Goldberger and O. D. Duncan (eds.), Structural Equation Models in the Social Sciences. New York: Seminar Press.

KUENNAPAS, T. and M. SELLIN (1964) Measurement of "Political" Preferences: A Comparison of Scaling Methods. University of Stockholm, Psychological Laboratory Report 172.

KUENNAPAS, T. and I. WIKSTROEM (1963) "Measurement of occupational preferences: A comparison of scaling methods." Perceptual and Motor Skills 17: 611-624.

LABOVITZ, S. (1970) "The assignment of numbers to rank order categories." American Sociological Review 35: 515-524.

LODGE, M. and B. TURSKY (1981) "The social-psychophysical scaling of political opinion," in B. Wegener (ed.), Social Attitudes and Psychophysical Measurement. Hillsdale, NJ: Erlbaum.

LODGE, M., D. CROSS, B. TURSKY, J. TANENHAUS, and R. REEDER (1976a) "The Psychophysical Scaling of Political Support in the 'Real World.'" Political Methodology 2: 159-182.

LODGE, M., D. CROSS, B. TURSKY, M. A. FOLEY, and H. FOLEY (1976b) "The calibration and cross-modal validation of ratio scales of political opinion in survey research." Social Science Research 5: 325-347.

LODGE, M., D. CROSS, B. TURSKY, and J. TANENHAUS (1975) "The psychophysical scaling and validation of a political support scale." American Journal of Political Science 19: 611-649.

LODGE, M., B. TURSKY, J. TANENHAUS, and D. CROSS (1974) The Development and Validation of Political Attitude Scales: A Psychophysical Approach. Laboratory for Behavioral Research, Report 2.

LUCE, R. D. (1959) "On the possible psychophysical laws." Psychological Review 66: 81-95.

MARKS, L. E. (1974) Sensory Processes: The New Psychophysics. New York: Academic Press.

MARKS, L. E. (1968) "Stimulus-range, number of categories, and the form of the category scale." American Journal of Psychology 81: 467-479.

NAMBOODIRI, N., L. F. CARTER, and H. M. BLALOCK, Jr. (1975) Applied Multivariate Analysis and Experimental Designs. New York: McGraw-Hill.

SARIS, W. (1980) "Linear structural relationships." Quality and Quantity 14: 205-224.

SELLIN, J. T. and M. E. WOLFGANG (1964) The Measurement of Delinquency. New York: John Wiley.

SHINN, A., Jr. (1974) "Relations between scales," in H. M. Blalock, Jr. (ed.), Measurement in the Social Sciences: Theories and Strategies. Chicago: Aldine.

SHINN, A., Jr. (1969) "An application of psychophysical scaling techniques to the measurement of national power." Journal of Politics 31: 932-951.

STEVENS, J. C., J. D. MACK, and S. S. STEVENS (1960) "Growth of sensation on seven continua as measured by force of handgrip." Journal of Experimental Psychology 59: 60-67.

STEVENS, S. S. (1975) Psychophysics: Introduction to its Perceptual, Neural, and Social Prospects. New York: John Wiley.

STEVENS, S. S. (1972) Psychophysics and Social Scaling. Morristown, NJ: General Learning Press.

STEVENS, S. S. (1969) "On predicting exponents for cross-modality matches." Perception & Psychophysics 6: 251-256.

STEVENS, S. S. (1966a) "A metric for the social consensus." Science 151: 530-541.

STEVENS, S. S. (1966b) "Matching functions between loudness and ten other continua." Perception & Psychophysics 1: 5-8.

STEVENS, S. S. (1957) "On the psychophysical law." Psychological Review 64: 153-181.

STEVENS, S. S. and E. GALANTER (1957) "Ratio scales and category scales for a dozen perceptual continua." Journal of Experimental Psychology 54: 377-411.

STEVENS, S. S. and M. GUIRAO (1963) "Subjective scaling of length and area and the matching of length to hardness and brightness." Journal of Experimental Psychology 59: 60-67.

TANENHAUS, J. and W. MURPHY (1981) "Patterns of public support for the Supreme Court: A panel study." Journal of Politics 43: 324-339.

TEGHTSOONIAN, M. and R. TEGHTSOONIAN (1965) "Seen and felt length." Psychonomic Science 3: 465-466.

TORGERSON, W. S. (1968) "Scaling." International Encyclopedia of the Social Sciences 14: 25-38. New York: Macmillan.

TUFTE, E. R. (1969) "Improving data analysis in political science." World Politics 21: 641-654.

WARD, L. M. (1972) "Category judgments of loudness in the absence of an experiment-induced identification function: Sequential effects and power-function fit." Journal of Experimental Psychology 94: 179-184.

WEGENER, B. (1981) "Fitting category of magnitude scales of opinion," in B. Wegener (ed.), Social Attitudes and Psychophysical Measurement. Hillsdale, NJ: Erlbaum.

WELCH, R. E., Jr. (1972) "The use of magnitude estimation in attitude scaling: Constructing a measure of political dissatisfaction." Social Science Quarterly 76-87.

WILSON, T. P. (1971) "Critique of ordinal variables," pp. 415-431 in H. M. Blalock, Jr. (ed.), Causal Models in the Social Sciences. Chicago: Aldine-Atherton.

MILTON LODGE is Professor of Political Science at the State University of New York at Stony Brook and co-director, with Bernard Tursky, of the Laboratory for Behavioral Research. His current research employs magnitude scaling within information processing models to study political belief systems. Despite this emphasis on magnitude scaling, some of his best friends use category scales. All the psychophysical scaling studies carried out by Stony Brook's Laboratory were funded by the Political Science Program of the National Science Foundation.

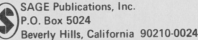

Quantitative Applications
in the Social Sciences

A SAGE UNIVERSITY PAPER SERIES

$4.00 each

SAGE PUBLICATIONS, INC.
P.O. BOX 5024
BEVERLY HILLS, CALIFORNIA 90210-0024

Place
Stamp
here